Political Science as Puzzle Solving

Interests, Identities, and Institutions in Comparative Politics

———

The post–Cold War world faces a series of defining global challenges: virulent forms of conflict, the resurgence of the market as the basis for economic organization, and the construction of democratic institutions.

The books in this series take advantage of the rich development of different approaches to comparative politics in order to offer new perspectives on these problems. The books explore the emerging theoretical and methodological synergisms and controversies about social conflict, political economy, and institutional development.

———

Political Science as Puzzle Solving

———

Bernard Grofman, Editor

Ann Arbor

THE UNIVERSITY OF MICHIGAN PRESS

2004   2003   2002   4   3   2

A CIP catalog record for this book is available from the British Library.

Library of Congress Cataloging-in-Publication Data

Political science as puzzle solving / Bernard Grofman, editor.
        p.   cm. — (Interests, identities, and institutions in
    comparative politics)
    Includes bibliographical references and index.
        ISBN 0-472-11176-0 (cloth : alk. paper) — ISBN 0-472-08723-1
    (pbk. : alk. paper)
        1. Comparative government.   2. Political Science—Decision
    making.   3. Rational choice theory.   I. Grofman, Bernard.   II. Series.
    JF51 .P625   2001
    320'.01'1356—dc21   00-010297

Contents

Acknowledgments

Earlier versions of several of the papers in this volume were first presented at the Conference on Rational Choice Approaches to Comparative Politics, funded by a grant from the National Science Foundation to Russell Dalton, Harry Eckstein, and Bernard Grofman (NSF SES # 91-13984). The conference, co-organized by Bernard Grofman and George Tsebelis, took place at UCI in May 22–23, 1992, under the sponsorship of the University of California, Irvine, Focused Research Program in Public Choice (now the UCI Interdisciplinary Graduate Concentration in Public Choice) and the University of California, Irvine, Focused Research Program on Democracy and Democratization (now the Center for the Study of Democracy). It was the sixth in a series of UCI conferences on topics in political economy and empirical democratic theory, the first of which was organized by Julius Margolis in 1982.* We would like to extend special thanks to Russell Dalton, then Chair of the UCI Focused Research Program on Democracy and Democratization and Amihai Glazer, then Director of the UCI Focused Research Program in Public Choice, for their help in making this original conference possible. I would also like to thank Carol Mershon for her help with this conference.

Earlier versions of four of the chapters in this volume have been published previously. Chapter 1 was originally published as Kaare Strøm, "The Presthus

*Papers from the second Irvine conference, *Information Pooling and Group Decision-Making* (B. Grofman and G. Owen, eds.), were published by JAI Press in 1986. Papers from the third conference, *The 'Federalist Papers' and the New Institutionalism* (B. Grofman and D. Wittman, eds.) were published by Agathon Press in 1989. Papers from the fifth conference were published in two volumes, *The Economic Approach to Politics* (K. R. Monroe, ed.), published by Harper-Collins in 1991, and *Information, Participation, and Choice: 'An Economic Theory of Democracy' in Perspective* (B. Grofman, ed.), published by the University of Michigan Press in 1993. Papers from the seventh conference, *Term Limits: Public Choice Perspectives* (B. Grofman, ed.), were published by Kluwer in 1996. Papers from the fourth conference, *Elections in Japan, Korea, and Taiwan under the Single Non-transferable Vote: Lessons from the Study of an Embedded Institution* (B. Grofman, S. C. Lee, E. A. Winckler, and B. Woodall, eds.), were published by the University of Michigan Press in 1999. Papers from the eighth conference, *The Single Transferable Vote in Ireland, Australia, and Malta* (S. Bowler and B. Grofman, eds.), were published in 2000.

Debate: Intraparty Politics and Bargaining Failure in Norway," *American Political Science Review* 88, no. 1 (March 1994): 112–27. Chapter 2 was originally published as Miriam Golden, "The Politics of Job Loss," *American Journal of Political Science* 36, no. 2 (May 1992): 408–30, reprinted by permission of the University of Wisconsin Press. Chapter 3 was originally published as Masaru Kohno, "Electoral Origins of Japanese Socialists' Stagnation," *Comparative Political Studies* 30, no. 1 (February 1997): 55–77, reprinted by permission of Sage Publications, Inc. Chapter 5 was originally published as George Tsebelis and Roland Stephen, "Monitoring Unemployment Benefits in Comparative Perspective," *Political Research Quarterly* 47, no. 4 (December 1994): 793–820, reprinted by permission of the University of Utah, copyright holder.

Introduction: The Joy of Puzzle Solving

Bernard Grofman

Political science, especially the field of comparative politics, has been torn between advocates of thick description and detailed knowledge of historical, cultural, and social context and those who argue the need for simplifying assumptions and formal modeling to make theoretical sense of a complex world. Personally, since I am, like my colleague, A Wuffle, a member of the California (drive-in) Church of the Incorrigibly Eclectic, I see no need to take an either-or stand in this debate.[1] I think both sides are right; or, alternatively, both sides are wrong—that is, the proof is in the pudding and not in abstract debate about methodology or epistemology. A key task for empirically oriented social scientists is to find interesting features of the world and try to tell us something insightful that will help us explain them/understand them better. If—whatever your methodology—you can do that, more power to you. If you can't, find another line of work.[2] Abstract debate about the epistemological and ontological merits or demerits of particular styles/types of explanation are, in my view, not especially enlightening.

A puzzle-solving approach can be a bridge between alternative methodological perspectives. A focus on solving concrete puzzles derived from empirical observation can force those whose methodological leanings are in the modeling direction to be attentive to real-world phenomena at the same time as it can force more ideographically oriented political scientists to look beyond the facts to theoretically grounded explanations of those facts. A puzzle-solving approach forces arguments about the explanatory power of certain (types of) theory to move away from debates about abstract concepts to real debates about real issues, in particular, the power of competing explanations to explain real-world puzzles.

This book offers five important puzzles—puzzles in comparative politics[3]—and looks at the solutions that certain political scientists have proposed for them.

In the first three chapters an author looks at the behavior of an individual or an organization such as trade union or political party that, at first blush, just doesn't seem to make sense: "Why would a political leader gamble on a vote of confidence that he didn't need to call and the failure of which would seriously harm his party's future prospects?" (the Kaare Strøm chapter); "Why would a trade union conduct a strike that it knows it can't win?" (the Miriam Golden chapter); "Why didn't the Japanese Socialist party modify its platform to attract more voters so as to give it a chance of holding power in Japan?" (the Masaru Kohno chapter). In these chapters the authors show that behavior that appears irrational is not really so once we understand the full context in which the behavior is embedded.

The fourth chapter, by Richard Anderson, takes its puzzles from a phenomenon that appears counterintuitive—indeed, virtually inexplicable. "How could a major empire (the Soviet empire) have dissolved so quickly?" Here the explanation involves an interesting new theory: the power of "decisive inaction."[4]

The last chapter (that by George Tsebelis and Roland Stephen) elaborates a formal model of equilibrium behavior in the social welfare system to consider the empirical puzzle "Why does increasing the unemployment benefits often appear not to significantly increase the attractiveness of the unemployment option?"

Outline of the Book

In chapter 1, Strøm's explanation of the seemingly irrational behavior by Norwegian party leaders shows how a too simplistic notion of what constitutes rational behavior can go wrong, namely, treating parties as unitary actors when they are not. He explains why a nonsocialist majority of four parties in Norway, each explicitly committed to dislodging a socialist government, twice failed to agree on a simple vote to that end. He shows that the interests of party leaders (and thus what is rational for them to do given their own career incentives) need not be identical to those of the party they represent. He also shows how sequential bargaining situations can give rise to errors in expectations that lead to errors in judgment.

In chapter 2, Golden explains differences in tactics between Italian and British automobile plant trade unions with similar histories of militancy facing similar threats of major layoffs (albeit layoffs cushioned by the promise of severance pay). Organized labor in Great Britain acceded to 30 percent layoffs at British Leyland without a strike, while Italian unions at Fiat engaged in a more than month-long strike that they lost, after which labor employment fell by a third over the next three years. Rejecting the five most often proposed explanations for the differences in outcomes in the two cases (e.g., the supposed greater influence of Italian shop stewards, or differences in political culture), Golden offers an institutional explanation focusing on differences in seniority rules. She argues that "militant resistance to job loss will . . . occur in situations without effective seniority systems."

In chapter 3, Masaru Kohno looks at why the Japanese Socialist Party (JSP) clung to its original leftist politics so long, despite the fact that the platforms they advocated made it impossible for them to achieve majority party status in Japan. After considering previous explanations for this self-defeating behavior, including the central role of labor in the JSP's campaign organization and the strength of key ideological concerns that apparently dominated electoral motives, Kohno suggests an alternative explanation. He links JSP policy choices to certain features of the single nontransferable vote system used for the lower chamber in the Japanese parliament from 1997 to 1994 that helped structure the nature of electoral incentives and constraints that affected party competition in Japan.

In chapter 4, Richard Anderson tackles the question of the fate of the Soviet Empire. How could sovietologists have so baldly missed the signs of its imminent dissolution? Was that collapse not really inevitable? How could the former Soviet Union have dissolved so quickly? Anderson offers a theory that ties the timing of the empire's fall to certain critical choices made by Premier Gorbachev, choices that Anderson characterizes as "decisive *in*actions." For Anderson, it was what Gorbachev did *not* do in response to certain crises (things that everyone in the Soviet Union expected him to do because they were the kinds of responses made by his predecessors in similar circumstances) that made the difference.

In chapter 5, George Tsebelis and Roland Stephen make use of the tools of game theory to study the changes in behavior that occur when one parameter of the social welfare system, the level of benefits to those out of work, is changed. Ceteris paribus, it would seem that increasing unemployment benefits should increase the attractiveness of the unemployment option. Yet they show that increased benefits seem to have only a limited effect on unemployment rates. Why? Tsebelis and Stephen's answer rests on an analysis of equilibrium behavior; they show that increasing the benefits will affect the behavior of those who monitor eligibility requirements and not just affect the calculations of potential beneficiaries. These changes in law enforcement activities may serve as a deterrent that in part offsets the seeming appeal of increased benefits.

Discussion

We may classify the chapters in this volume in terms of the generality of the phenomenon that is being explained, ranging from attempts to explain either the behavior or the consequences of the behavior of particular actors in a given country (party leaders in the case of Strøm, Anderson, and Kohno) or types of actors (trade unions in the case of Golden) to explanations of behavior cast in very abstract and general terms (e.g., Tsebelis and Stephen's model of a welfare system and the equilibrium response of its components to changes in particular parameters such as benefit level).

Another useful way to characterize the chapters in this volume is terms of categories derived from the literature on the art of the mystery.[5] Mysteries can be seen as generally falling into three categories: "whodunits," "howdunits," and "whydunits." In a whodunit the central issue is simply pinning down who committed the crime; whodunits are what most of us think of when we think about mystery stories.[6] In contrast, in howdunits and whydunits we often know the identity of the perpetrator from the start. In the former, the emphasis is on exactly how the deed was pulled off.[7] In the latter, we are interested in probing the psychology of the criminal and the motivation and background of the crime.[8] We may think of the chapters by Golden, Kohno, and Strøm as in large part whydunits, seeking to explaining the otherwise mysterious (because apparently irrational) motivations of particular actors; while the other two chapters can be seen as combining the concerns of the traditional whodunit (perhaps, for the Anderson chapter, better labeled as a "whatdunit," i.e., identifying a mechanism—the villain—that done the deed), with the howdunit's concern for the exact nature of that explanatory mechanism.

Since all of the work in this volume can be thought of as falling loosely within the rational choice tradition, still another way to think about the chapters in this volume is in terms of a continuum ranging from what is often called "soft" rational choice (i.e., verbal analyses that draw on the idea that people do things for reasons and, if we can understand their reasons, we can help explain their behavior), to the intermediate category of work that looks at game-theoretic equilibria in particular concrete situations, to the extreme of "hard" rational choice, that is, purely mathematical results divorced from any immediate empirical context. Because this is about the solving of empirical puzzles, none of the chapters in this volume fall on the extreme "hard" end of this spectrum. The Golden, Anderson, and Kohno chapters clearly fall into the category of "soft" rational choice, and the Strøm chapter and the Tsebelis and

Stephen chapter are in the intermediate category in that they do offer explicitly game-theoretic models and look for equilibria.

However, as my late colleague Harry Eckstein (personal communication, 1992) noted, it seems perverse to label as "soft" work that seeks to test models empirically, while reserving the label "hard" for theorem-proving papers whose mathematical results may, in fact, have no empirically testable implications. Even though mathematical and statistical techniques can be invaluable to their practitioners, social science is not a branch of mathematics (but, of course, neither is physics or chemistry).[9] Thus insofar as "hard science" is thought to be better than soft science (and hardheadedness preferred, of course, to gullibility), unlike the case of Hamilton and Madison successfully stealing the name "federalists" that more properly belonged to their "antifederalist" (*sic!*) opponents, I regard the theft of the term "hard" by theorem-provers to be unfortunate. By reserving the term "hard" for purely mathematical work that may have little or no direct empirical application, it denigrates the contributions of those who are trying to make sense of the world.[10]

The original title of the 1992 conference that inspired this volume was "Rational Choice Approaches to Comparative Politics." Since that conference, much important work has been done applying rational choice ideas in comparative politics (see, e.g., Bates et al. 1998a), but the debate about the merits and demerits of rational choice theory in political science has also heated up considerably. There are at least five edited books specifically about the value of rational choice approaches and several journals (including *Critical Review, Rationality and Society,* and the *Journal of Theoretical Politics,* which have had mini-symposia on this topic); and, of course, Green and Shapiro (1994) have written a book-length diatribe against Downsian and other Public Choice models.[11] While the original draft of this volume had some chapters on the nature of rational choice theory, these chapters have been dropped from this volume[12] in light of how much has already been written in what seems to me to be too often a sterile and boring exercise in abstract argumentation.[13] Not only do many critiques of rational choice theory involve attacks on straw men, or criticisms of empirical work based on standards of evidence and explanation that are set impossibly high and don't bear any resemblance to how social scientists (rational choice and otherwise) actually conduct research; but, most important, debate has had, as far as I can tell, *zero* effect on the kind of research that people actually do. Thus, the aim of the present volume has been to focus on puzzle solving, not on rational choice per se.

Moreover, classifying the chapters that appear in this volume into "softer" or "harder" forms of rational choice modeling can be quite misleading since, in each chapter, it is the empirical puzzle that drives the enterprise, not the methodology per se, and the chapters illustrate that country-specific knowledge and analytic tools are, as Barry Weingast (1996) nicely put it, "complementary rather than competing" sources of understanding. Golden, for example, makes use of a model that emphasizes institution-driven incentive structures[14] and is able to integrate the perspectives derived from that modeling with her knowledge of British and Italian trade union history. Kohno's chapter, too, seeks to integrate the insights of formal theory with insights derived from detailed institutional analysis of a traditional sort in reexamining the motivations underlying the policy choices made by the Japanese Socialist Party.

To come full circle, my own preferred way to think about all of the chapters in this volume is in terms of their similarities. They all pose important puzzles and seek to answer them. The five chapters deal with voting behavior, interest groups, regime change, government formation, and public policy. Our chapters span northern and southern Europe and the former Soviet Union. How successful a job each of the chapters in this volume does in addressing the puzzle it purports to explain readers must, of course, judge for themselves. But regardless of the merits or demerits of particular chapters in this volume (or in the planned companion volume that discusses six puzzles about U.S. congressional elections), I hope to persuade the reader that it is useful to think about social science as, in good part, a puzzle-solving activity.

Along those lines, let me now briefly address some of the questions that have probably already occurred to the reader in the form of five likely objections to my proposal to make puzzle solving more central in thinking about what it means to do social science.

1.   Is puzzle solving too limited in that it allows us only to deal with trivial or minor issues? Here, I would argue that puzzles (like research topics in general) come in all sizes, from very narrow and fact-specific (e.g., why did persons X, Y, and Z engage in acts D, E, and F, e.g., why did a prime minister and his chief opponents behave in a particular way in a particular crisis?), to mid-range puzzles (e.g., why is the U.S. Senate in the post–World War II period more Republican than the U.S. House?), to more big-picture puzzles (e.g., why do some societies where women have made major advances in the workplace still have so few women legislators? Or, why do unions strike when they have no chance of winning? Or, bigger still, how could the Soviet empire have dissolved so quickly?).

2.   Is puzzle solving a distraction from the real job of building general theory? Here, I would first note that puzzle solving is only one of many possible

styles of research and that, while I don't think there's been enough of it in the discipline, that is certainly not to say that every article or book (or even most) needs to be written within a puzzle-solving framework. The need for general theory building is as strong as ever. But, I would argue that the problem of theory building is a general problem of making work cumulate and interlock, and that while puzzle solving offers no readier solutions to that problem than any other approach, it can lead to the development of general theory, especially as we come to grips with particular puzzles that have implications beyond a particular time and place. To move beyond abstraction and irrelevance, theories have to confront concrete facts and seek to explain then.

3. Is puzzle solving necessarily so selective in the facts that its chooses for its puzzle and the facts that it uses for its explanation that the explanations it offers are of little use? Here, I would argue that all work is selective, even the thickest of descriptions. Any model needs to be selective in a good way, that is, to focus on a relative handful of factors that have substantial explanatory power. If we look at any theorizing, whether it be Huntington's clash of cultures or Wallerstein's world system theory, to name two approaches that are not regarded as "rational choice" in nature, it seems obvious to me (as I suspect it does to most readers) how remarkably selective they are in the factors they regard as critical, and in their discussion of the phenomenon they are trying to explain. I am a pragmatist. The value of a theory must be judged in the "bang for the buck," for example, the extent to which a sparse model has a broad scope.

4. Is puzzle solving so limited in the way that it explains a given phenomenon that it offers not real explanations but only pseudoexplanations that beg the question of true causation? For example, Anderson's chapter tells us how Gorbachev's decisive *in*actions allowed the Soviet empire to dissolve so quickly, but it is easy to claim that Anderson does not address the (perhaps allegedly much more important question) of how Gorbachev came to be in a position to act (or rather, fail to act) as he did. Here, I would emphasize that any explanation takes some facts/phenomena as given, even though for other purposes those very phenomena would themselves need explanation. No explanation is ever complete. There is nothing unique to rational choice approaches or puzzle-solving approaches in having this limitation. To put it simply, it is often much more straightforward to discuss the validity of a given explanation than it is to debate, in the abstract, what the properties of a good explanation must be.

Most social scientists would agree that any explanation must be judged in the context of what it is that it is trying to explain, that any explanation must be judged in the context of competing explanations, and that any explanation must be judged in terms of the kinds of evidence it offers and the accuracy of the description it gives of what it is that is being explained. We need not resolve questions such the limitations of the nomological model—questions perhaps better left to the philosophers of science—to decide when we have, in social science terms, a reasonable explanation for a phenomenon such as, say, variations in the proportion of women in national parliaments.[15]

5.   Is puzzle solving just another name for rational choice? In a word, my answer to that question is no. While I count myself a "reasonable choice" modeler and all the essays in this volume are more or less "rational choice" in tone, there is nothing whatsoever in the puzzle-solving approach that requires that the answer to the puzzle be a game-theoretic equilibrium or even a story about preferences and constraints on choice. In fact, some of the papers that my students or I have written that are puzzle-oriented offer solutions that are explicitly institutional but not incentive-driven (e.g., Thomas Brunell's explanation [1999] of why the Senate has been more Republican than the House), and there's nothing to say that the best solution to some puzzle won't involve, for example, political culture (e.g., Putnam's work on North-South differences in Italy). In some particular instance, we may approach a puzzle inspired by ideas from rational choice theory—or we may not; we may make use of formal modeling to help us solve puzzles—or we may not. Which methodological ax has been sharpened is not the issue. Insight into a problem is what counts.

I would like to believe that proposing we focus more on concrete puzzles, and showing examples of chapters that do so, might actually influence the research choices of a next generation of graduate students. None of the standard methodological treatises or "scope and methods" primers I ever read treated puzzle solving as something central to what social science is all about, and I have deliberately written this introduction in a rather provocative fashion (emphasizing the theme of puzzle solving and whodunits, whydunits, and howdunits) with that aim in mind. Looking at what we do in concrete puzzle-solving terms forces empirical relevance, discourages methodological dogmatism, and can convey a spirit of excitement to our students.[16] Puzzle solving can be fun.[17]

NOTES

1. Cf. Collier 1999.
2. For some who find empirical work too daunting, there is always theology.

3. In a companion volume, *Six Puzzles about Congressional Elections,* my coauthors (Thomas Brunell and William Koetzle) and I consider questions such as: "Why do we see virtually certain midterm loss in the House, but not in the Senate?" "Why has split-ticket voting exhibited a pattern of rise, then fall, and, most recently, rise again?" and "Why have the Republicans generally done better in recent decades for the Senate than for the House?"

4. Another example of this type of conundrum—"Why did Italian cabinets topple with great rapidity but the politicians who toppled with them return to power again and again?"—is discussed in Mershon 1996.

5. I have been reading about one mystery story a day for nearly forty years and I own over 5,000 titles. Mostly I read mysteries for relaxation, but I also read them because I am interested in puzzles.

6. Recall, for example, the old Perry Mason courtroom dramas on television where we learn the identity of the criminal when he or she is trapped by Mason into an incriminating confession on the witness stand (or sometimes, even more implausibly, from their place in the back of the courtroom watching the trial).

7. See, e.g., the locked-room mysteries of John Dickson Carr, or the television mysteries solved by Columbo where we know who the killer is and Columbo, himself, intuits the identity of the killer very early in the program, but then has to break the killer's alibi.

8. See, e.g., some of the psychological novels of Ruth Rendell.

9. That said, as I have written elsewhere (Grofman 1993c), I regard game theory to be as central a tool to political science as, say, calculus, is to physics. However, I strongly reject the implicit or explicit view espoused by some modelers that anything that lacks a result about a game-theoretic equilibrium cannot be a major contribution to social science.

10. As to whether it is harder to prove a theorem than to do good empirical work, in my view, that depends upon the nature of the theorem and on how good the empirical work happens to be. Also, some people's talents lie in one direction rather than another.

11. My own contributions to the debate about the empirical contributions of Public Choice approaches include Grofman 1993a, 1993c, and 1996; see also various essays in Grofman 1993b, including my introduction to that volume. In this debate, Green and Shapiro (1994) and other critics of rational choice have been aided by the arrogance of some of the more dogmatic rational choice modelers who sometimes appear to confuse technical elegance or the level of mathematical difficulty required for a proof with the degree to which a result helps us make sense of the world.

12. One of these proposed chapters, by my colleague, A Wuffle, on his approach to "reasonable choice theory," has subsequently been published as Wuffle 1999 and deals with some of the more general issues related to rational choice bashing. Although written partly tongue-in-cheek (as is the case for all Wuffle publications), Wuffle (1999) expresses views which I strongly share. In particular, Wuffle (1999) argues, inter alia, that

There is no such thing as *the* rational choice model of any given phenomena, only *a* rational choice model; different models are based on different assumptions. Empirical science is about testing competing model*s*. Just as God is in the details, so is the power of rational choice in the secondary assumptions. Arguing in the abstract about which phenomena can or cannot be explained by rational choice models is not useful; indeed, arguing *in the absence of considered evidence* about which phenomena can or cannot be explained by (rational choice) models is downright stupid. Empirical science is about *testing* competing models. Demonstrating that some particular phenomenon cannot be well accounted for by some particular rational choice model demonstrates only that some particular rational choice model cannot explain that particular phenomenon; such a demonstration cannot invalidate the search for rational choice explanations of behavior. Hence, for example, [the failure of decisive voter models of] turnout cannot be "the paradox that ate rational choice theory." Demonstrating that some particular phenomenon cannot be well accounted for by some particular rational choice model may be of value to the advancement of science (à la Popper's falsification thesis), but, contra Popper, science advances most by what comes to be known not by what is shown to be false. Hence, debunking some particular rational choice model is of limited value unless one has something better to put in its place. Empirical *science* is about testing competing models.

Wuffle also asserts:

Saying that behavior is rational is not the same thing as saying that it is perfect; what is rational to being q at time t is a function of circumstances and information. What may be rational for being q at time t, may not be rational for being q at time $t + 1$, given that being's new circumstances and information. What may be rational for being q at time t, given that being's circumstances and information, may not be apparent to an observer who isn't walking in that being's shoes. [Also], [f]ew people do things for only one reason.

13. That is certainly not to say that nothing useful has been said in this debate.

14. Other authors who have looked at the strike decision have also emphasized how seeming irrationalities can be explained in the context of expected longer-run consequences of strikes on the labor-management bargaining game. Sometimes unions strike with no chance of victory, since unions that forgo strike activity will find it substantially harder to withstand pressures from management. There must be a credible strike threat, and that may require actually engaging in strike activity, even if unsuccessfully.

15. An insightful discussion of the properties of a good explanation, albeit one focused on evaluating the merits of particular analytical narratives, may be found in Bates et al. 1998b, 14–18. See also Wuffle 1999.

16. Here, I would note some interesting parallels between the approach outlined in this introduction and the recent work on "analytical narratives" by scholars such as Bob Bates and Margaret Levi (see esp. Bates et al. 1998a)—work that I hold in high regard. While this work is much more explicitly historical, like the puzzle-solving approach, it is very concrete in its desire to account for particular events or outcomes. Indeed, the authors see their approach as intended to occupy a "complex middle ground between nomothetic and idiographic approaches" (Bates et al. 1998b, 12). Also, while its focus on choices and decisions, and stress on viewing institutions as "subgame-

perfect equilibria," eschew the kind of methodological eclecticism that I have espoused, Bates and his coauthors are in no way guilty of the kind of dogmatism found among some rational choice theorists. In particular, they view their work as a "complement to, rather than a substitute for, structural and macro-level analyses" (Bates et al. 1998b, 13). However, despite my strong sympathy for their attempt to "locate and explore particular mechanisms that shape the interplay between strategic actors and thereby generate outcomes" (1998b, 12), which finds resonance in my own previous work on the effects of electoral systems (see esp. Davidson and Grofman 1994), and even though I would fully agree that actors do try to reason backward to anticipate the likely consequences of their actions, I would wish to enter a caveat about the emphasis of the analytical narratives approach on insights derived from equilibrium results. However, detailed discussion of this issue would take us well beyond the scope of this introduction.

17. I wouldn't be a political scientist myself if I didn't find doing social science a lot of fun.

Chapter 1

Why Did the Norwegian Conservative Party Shoot Itself in the Foot?

Kaare Strøm

Electoral politics moves in cycles, which are sometimes short and sometimes long. In Norway, the Conservative party was the major victor of the late 1970s and early 1980s. It has been in continuous decline, however, since the mid-1980s. In the early 1980s, it polled close to a third of the popular vote and challenged Labor for the position of Norway's dominant party. By the Storting (Parliament) election of 1997, however, the Conservatives had fallen to fourth place, and polls taken in the subsequent months put the party at barely more than 10 percent of the electorate.

The timing and causes of such cyclical shifts are often obscure. In the case of the Norwegian Conservative party, however, we can date the beginning of the party's precipitous decline with a good deal of accuracy. Though the party had suffered a minor reverse in the 1985 election, a much more dramatic decline set in just after the dramatic events associated with the farm bill debate of 1987. This decline has kept the party out of executive office for all but one of the ensuing years, and it has led to widespread speculation that the party may be redundant and indeed moribund.

The most intriguing aspect of this development is that the wounds of the Norwegian Conservative party were so much self-inflicted, a direct result of the party's failure to unseat the Labor party's minority government and replace it with a bourgeois coalition of the sort that had ruled Norway between 1983 and 1986. These events, and the calculations that went into the disastrously self-destructive behavior of the Conservative party, are the topics of this chapter.

Bourgeois Coalescence and the "Presthus Debacle"

On June 12, 1987, the Norwegian Storting rejected two separate no-confidence motions against the Labor party government headed by Gro Harlem Brundtland.

The nonsocialist majority of four parties, each explicitly committed to dislodging Brundtland's government, twice failed to agree on a simple vote to that end. The dreams of Conservative leader Rolf Presthus, the designated prime ministerial candidate of the nonsocialist parties, never materialized, and his party was humiliated.

The causes of this debacle are interesting for a number of reasons. First, the outcome was one that none of the principal players most preferred and few anticipated. Four parties, all explicitly committed to a change of government and collectively a legislative majority, twice failed to oust a minority government. Moreover, two of these parties, the Center party and especially the Conservatives, set the agenda in ways that left them distinctly worse off. The Presthus debacle underscores our limited understanding of bargaining failure in coalition politics. It demonstrates constraints on the ability of political parties to make enforceable agreements, as well as the importance of information and sequence in interparty negotiations. Finally, the events of June 1987 show that parties differ in the objectives they bring to coalition bargaining. To account for such differences in party objectives, we have to consider the constraints of politics within parties, especially the consequences of intraparty delegation regimes.

In this analysis, I first discuss the causes of bargaining failure, as well as the implications for coalition theory, then describe in greater detail the events of June 1987. I construct an initial game-theoretic representation of these events, derive various solutions, and test their adequacy. In order to solve the remaining puzzles, I then introduce a more complex account of party behavior, taking into account information uncertainties and intraparty constraints. I apply this framework to the various phases of the Presthus debacle in order to illuminate the behavior of the critical players. In the conclusion, I summarize the lessons of the Presthus debacle for the study of government coalitions.

Bargaining Failure and Coalition Theory

The making and breaking of interparty coalitions are dramatic and decisive events in parliamentary democracies. And although the study of coalition behavior has long been one of systematic, rigorous, and often formalized comparative inquiry, there are still significant lacunae in our knowledge. As students of coalition politics have pointed out, we know much less about coalition termination than we do about formation, and there is next to no systematic knowledge of what happens in between, that is, about the process of coalition governing (Laver and Shepsle 1990a).

Bargaining Failure and Selection Bias

Even the study of coalition formation is curiously incomplete. Empirical studies almost exclusively focus on coalitions that have actually formed, that is, on *successful* coalition bargaining. The sordid tales of bargaining failure are rarely told. But if our interest is in coalition bargaining itself, then this practice results in selection bias, which may distort our understanding to the extent that unsuccessful bargaining situations systematically differ from successful ones (Geddes 1990). By restricting our observations to cases of successful bargaining, we obtain samples that systematically misrepresent the likelihood of securing such agreements. If our interest is in coalition stability, for example, the effect of neglecting bargaining failures may be to systematically underrepresent the least favorable conditions for durable coalescence.

Information and Bargaining Failure

The principal reason coalition bargaining fails may be information uncertainty, which indeed has been a key concern in coalition theory since its inception. In his seminal work, Riker (1962) argued that information uncertainty could lead to deviations from his size principle, such as the formation of oversized coalitions, a thesis later elaborated by Dodd (1976). Luebbert took issue with this argument, claiming that "rationalist theory greatly overstates the role of information uncertainty" (1983, 242). In the face of bargaining failures like the Presthus debacle, Luebbert's dismissal seems too categorical, though he may have been right in suggesting that coalition theorists traditionally have emphasized the *wrong kinds* of information uncertainty. Riker and Dodd, for example, focused on uncertainty as to the weights (i.e., the number of parliamentary votes) and prior moves of other players (Dodd 1976, 40–47), whereas incomplete information about payoffs or feasible strategy sets may be the more critical uncertainties. In other words, the players in parliamentary bargaining are more likely to be uninformed about each other's options and objectives than about agreements and bids that already exist. In the Presthus debacle, as we shall see, the Conservatives and the Center party knew perfectly well how many seats the Progress party commanded. They were much less sure about how the latter weighed the costs and benefits of supporting their no-confidence motion.

Constraints and Intraparty Politics

Information uncertainty in coalition bargaining may in large part be a function of intraparty politics. Party leaders may know each other's personal preferences and yet be less than fully informed about the discretion each enjoys vis-à-vis his respective party. This problem goes to the heart of the assumption that parties bargain as unitary actors, a prevalent, though increasingly questioned, stylization in studies of cabinet coalitions (Laver and Schofield 1990; Laver and Shepsle 1990b; Luebbert 1986). It is often more fruitful to think of party leaders as agents of their respective parliamentary or extraparliamentary parties (their principals) in coalition bargaining. Because of variation in delegation regimes, party leaders may be constrained in different ways in these negotiations. Such constraints may strongly affect outcomes, and when bargaining fails, it may be because of how the hands of the agents are tied.

Institutions and Bargaining Models

Political institutions may also play an important part in bargaining failure. Coalition theory has traditionally paid little attention to the rules under which bargaining takes place (see, however, Pridham 1986; Strøm, Budge, and Laver 1994). Such rules may regulate the mandate of the formateur or informateur, the sequence of negotiations, or the set of parties with which this person is permitted to negotiate. Another important factor that has rarely been systematically considered is the effect of time constraints on coalition bargaining. Situations of extreme time pressure may be particularly likely to cause information uncertainty and to occasion delegation problems that impede effective party oversight. Indeed, the time pressures associated with the impending parliamentary recess significantly impinged on the negotiations resulting in the Presthus debacle.

The complex set of factors that might facilitate bargaining failure is not adequately captured in the traditional study of government coalitions. It theoretically has relied mainly on cooperative coalition theory, whose predicted outcomes are entirely preference-induced or, in Riker's (1980) words, "equilibria of tastes." The object has been to *characterize* a set of equilibria, generically large and unstable, without recourse to ad hoc institutional assumptions, which are indeed difficult to incorporate into this body of theory. Such considerations as information uncertainty, constraints, and sequential moves can much more adequately be addressed within the theory of noncooperative games. A disadvantage of noncooperative game theory is that its potential complexity may jeopardize parsimony of explanation. Yet, in exploring the Presthus debacle, we shall see that even very simple noncooperative models can generate significant insights. These considerations suggest that the emerging literature applying noncooperative games can make fruitful contributions to the study of multiparty coalition bargaining (see, e.g., Austen-Smith and Banks 1988; Baron 1991, 1993).

Presthus and the Events of June 1987

The Presthus debacle ended a lengthy effort by the Norwegian Conservative party and its sometime allies to resurrect the nonsocialist coalition that had governed Norway from 1965 to 1971 and again between 1983 and 1986 (see Strøm 1990b; Strøm and Leipart 1993).[1] In May 1986 Kåre Willoch's coalition, which had been reduced to a minority government in the September 1985 election, resigned after losing a bill to increase gasoline taxes to offset the precipitous decline in government oil revenues. Gro Harlem Brundtland formed a precarious Labor minority government facing a nonsocialist legislative majority. Upon his resignation as prime minister, Willoch also passed the chairmanship of the Conservative party to his handpicked successor, Rolf Presthus, who had previously served as Willoch's finance minister.

Presthus's chief concern was to reconstruct the bourgeois coalition.[2] As finance minister, he had distinguished himself as an effective facilitator of interparty compromise, and largely for this reason, the Conservatives had elected him as their leader. Since the Conservative party, with 50 seats in the 157-member Storting, was almost twice as large as its two potential partners combined, Presthus was also the designated prime ministerial candidate of the three "coalitional" parties: the Center party (with 12 seats), the Christian People's party (with 16 seats), and the Conservatives. His first opportunity to gain office arose in October 1986 during the debate on the budget presented by finance minister Gunnar Berge. The failure of this so-called autumn hunting season became apparent on October 28, when the three coalitional parties abandoned their attempt to reach a budget accord. The Labor government survived, and the breakdown of these negotiations immediately led to mutual blaming and name-calling by Conservative and Center party representatives.

The next chance to defeat Brundtland arrived during the following spring session, when there were two legislative opportunities for joint nonsocialist action: the revised national budget, which contained an agenda for long-term economic policies such as taxation, and the government's farm bill. During April and May 1987, the three parties began to coordinate their policies in these two areas, amid extensive media speculation about the prospects for a change of government. The leaders of all three parties encouraged such speculations by issuing optimistic, though duly ambiguous, public declarations.

As negotiations reached a definitive phase in early June, the different designs of the three parties became more evident. The Center party and the Conservatives in particular had distinctly different preferences over the different potential censure motions that were discussed. One possibility was a general motion of no confidence unrelated to any particular issue. The second and third options were no-confidence motions attached to a farm bill amendment (to increase agricultural subsidies) or to a minority report on the revised national budget (to provide tax relief). The Center party, with its distinctly rural and agricultural constituency, strongly favored the farm bill option, whereas the Conservatives equally clearly preferred the third (the revised national budget). The position of the Christian People's party (KRF) was less clear. On June 5, party leader Kjell Magne Bondevik signaled a weak preference for the option favored by the Conservatives. However, the KRF leader seemed most anxious to maximize the likelihood of passage. Bondevik was concerned that, since the three coalitional parties collectively controlled only 78 of the 157 seats in the Storting, they needed the two votes of the pivotal right-wing Progress party. The six Left Socialist party (SV) members had to be counted upon to support Labor's 71 representatives in any showdown with the bourgeois opposition.

Although the three coalitional parties needed the Progressive vote, they were not prepared to enter any binding agreement with a party many considered irresponsible and extremist. The question, therefore, was what sort of no-confidence motion Carl I. Hagen, the Progress party leader, would support without a quid pro quo. Hagen had explicitly promised to support a general no-confidence motion. He could also be counted upon to sympathize with a proposal to lower taxes, since tax relief was his party's principal policy concern. Higher farm subsidies, on the other hand, were hardly an issue for which the Progress party would muster any enthusiasm. On a no-confidence motion attached to this bill, Hagen would therefore be forced to choose between his preferences for a nonsocialist government and lower farm spending.

Negotiations between the three coalitional parties increased their pace through June 8, as the end of the parliamentary session was rapidly approaching. After June 12, the Storting would be in recess for four months, with local and regional elections in September. It eventually became clear that the Center party would insist on attaching the no-confidence motion to a farm bill amendment. The Center party's insistence, which left no room for concessions, set the agenda for the battle over the Labor government's life. The Christian People's party, with few stakes in farm policy or tax relief, quickly accepted the Center party's policy demands. With recess less than a week away, the national executive committee of the Conservative party eventually caved in on June 8 and accepted farm subsidies as the key to a nonsocialist government. This agreement was cemented on July 10, when the three parties' members of the agriculture committee drafted a joint no-confidence motion calling for higher agricultural appropriations.

The pivotal Progress party decision came on June 11, the penultimate day of the Storting's spring session and the day before the parliamentary vote. Precisely at 7:30 P.M., Progress party leader Carl I. Hagen gave a press conference, which was broadcast live at the top of the prime-time television news hour. Hagen's speech, in which he disclosed that the Progress party would not topple Brundtland at the cost of budget-busting farm subsidies, was an immense publicity hit. In chastising the other bourgeois parties for their irresponsibility and opportunism, Hagen managed to project fiscal and ethical integrity. And while he rejected the farm bill amendment, Hagen explicitly committed his party to a general no-confidence vote against Brundtland.

The next day the final act unfolded. Arne Alsåker Spilde, a Conservative member of the Agriculture committee, formally introduced the no-confidence motion. At about 9:30 P.M., the Storting defeated Spilde's motion by a vote of 80 to 77, as the Progress party and the Socialist Left cast their lots with Labor.[3] Approximately one hour later the legislators faced a second no-confidence motion, pressed by Conservative parliamentary leader Jan P. Syse and expressly built on the joint minority report of the three coalitional parties on the revised national budget. This motion was supported also by the Christian People's party and allegedly drafted in large part by Kjell Magne Bondevik (*Dagbladet,* June 17, 1987). After a bitter debate, Syse's motion failed by a larger margin (89 to 68) than Spilde's (*Stortingstidende* 1986–87, 4082–4214). In the end, the Center party voted against Syse's measure even though it was based on the party's own financial program. These defeats left the nonsocialist parties embarrassed and bitterly divided, while Socialist Left parliamentary leader Hanna Kvanmo gloated over "this historic moment: the burial of nonsocialist cooperation" (Rommetvedt 1991, 208).[4] Kvanmo was temporarily correct, since the nonsocialist parties would make no further coalition efforts until after the September 1989 election.

The Presthus debacle also took its human toll. When the Storting finally took its summer recess at 2:30 A.M., Center party deputy leader Anne Enger

Lahnstein remained seated in the empty chamber, quietly weeping over the humiliations her party had suffered during the acrimonious debate. Yet the hardest blows fell on Rolf Presthus himself. More than anybody else, he had been the architect of nonsocialist cooperation, and as the bourgeois prime ministerial candidate, he would also have been its main beneficiary. The failure of Presthus's efforts quickly led to calls for his resignation as Conservative leader. In September, the Conservatives suffered a staggering defeat in the local and regional elections, and Presthus immediately tendered his resignation. Four months later he was dead at the age of 51, felled by a massive heart attack.

Game Representation

This complex and puzzling Presthus debacle involved a variety of players, as summarized in the appendix. The purpose of this article is to test the explanatory power of simple noncooperative game models against these puzzles and complexities. I shall do so by exploring first a very simple set of assumptions, and then enriching these models as the task at hand requires. The interaction between these parties can be divided into two subgames: an unstructured bargaining game up through June 10, which set the agenda for a subsequent, structured endgame over the following two days. My strategy will be to analyze these games in reverse order, beginning with the endgame and then using its solutions to understand the prior bargaining game. Figure 1 represents the endgame in extensive form, with each of the critical parties as a player. The game tree contains three decision nodes, illustrated by circles at which the player is identified by the first letter in that party's Norwegian acronym. These decision nodes represent choices faced by the three critical parties and the sequence in which they were confronted. Note that this sequence corresponds to the order in which the parties had to make their actual decisions, and not to the formal voting procedure in the Storting. The branches lead from the starting node to four different end nodes (outcomes) identified by roman numerals. End node III represents the actual outcome.

For simplicity, figure 1 excludes parties whose moves were taken for granted by all players. Thus, it was common knowledge that Labor and the Socialist Left would vote against any no-confidence motion, that the Christian People's party would support any feasible censure motion, and that the Progressives would join any tax-related or general motion pressed by the Conservatives. The parties in question had, in essence, precommitted themselves to these strategies.

The agenda reconstructed in figure 1 had been set by the previous bargain-

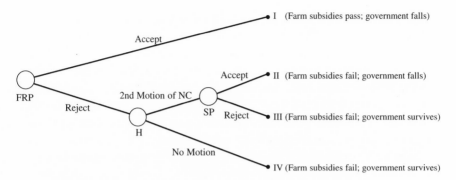

Figure 1. Extensive-form representation of Presthus endgame.
(FRP = Progress party; H = Conservative party; SP = Center party.)

ing between the three coalitional parties. The sequence of moves is as follows. The Progress party (FRP) first decides whether to accept the farm bill amendment. If it does, the government is defeated (outcome I). If, on the other hand, the Progress party rejects this no-confidence motion, the Brundtland government's fate depends on the further moves by the other bourgeois parties. The Conservatives (H) then have to decide, presumably after consultations with the Christian People's party (KRF), whether or not to press their own motion of no confidence, based on the national budget. If they do not, the game ends at outcome IV. If they do press a second no-confidence motion, and assuming the support of the Christian People's party and the Progressives, the Center party (SP) has a second opportunity to dislodge Brundtland (outcome II). If the Center party rejects the second (Syse) censure motion, however, the outcome is III.[5]

Figure 1 represents this game in its simplest form by assuming perfect and certain information.[6] The expectations concerning the outcome of this endgame are derived from simple noncooperative game models. The equilibrium concept is subgame perfect Nash, which implies that in equilibrium no player has any incentive unilaterally to deviate from his strategy, and that this condition applies in every subgame as well (see Fudenberg and Tirole 1991; Rasmusen 1989).[7] In the extensive-form representation in figure 1, solutions are found through backward induction from the end nodes (outcomes I through IV).

Party Objectives

In order to solve this game we need to stipulate how each party evaluates each of the outcomes to which each of its choices may lead. It is clearly desirable to derive these preferences from general assumptions about the motives ("objective functions") of the players, here the relevant Norwegian party leaders. For this purpose I rely on three common and parsimonious models of competitive party behavior, derived from the literatures on electoral competition and coalition formation: (1) the office-seeking party, (2) the policy-seeking party, and (3) the vote-seeking party (Strøm 1990a). The *office-seeking* party seeks to maximize its control of public office and the spoils it derives from such control (see Leiserson 1968; Riker 1962). The *policy-seeking* party instead maximizes its impact on public policy (Axelrod 1970; Budge and Laver 1986; de Swaan 1973). Finally, the *vote-seeking* party seeks to maximize its support in future electoral contests (Downs 1957; Cox 1987). We can give these general models concrete meaning in this Norwegian case by specifying the aspects of the various outcomes that are relevant to each party under each behavioral assumption. This specification is obviously a tall order, and again I simplify as much as possible.

Policy Preferences

If parties were pure policy-seekers, then what would be the critical aspect of the game outcome? As shown in table 1, the only issue clearly riding on the June 1987 negotiations was agricultural policy. On June 6, Center party leader Johan J. Jakobsen had taken pains to stress that a potential nonsocialist government should not be expected to pursue economic policies significantly different from those of its predecessor (Rommetvedt 1991, 196). I hence assume that policy-seeking parties would vote according to their preferences on the farm bill, and that they would be indifferent between outcomes that are equivalent as far as farm policy is concerned.[8] Other issues enter their calculations only secondarily, in the sense that if forced to vote on such issues (e.g., the national budget), parties (strictly) prefer voting in accordance with their program to voting against it.[9]

TABLE 1.   Properties of Different Outcomes of Endgame

Property	Outcome			
	I	II	III	IV
Government falls?	Y	Y	N	N
Farm subsidies pass?	Y	N	N	N
Coalition parties agree?	Y	Y	N	Y
Center party policy-consistent?	Y	Y	N	Y

Assumption P1:   The Center party prefers any outcome in which its farm bill amendment passes to any outcome in which it fails. Thus, it prefers outcome I to all others. Secondarily, if forced to vote on its national budget policy, the party prefers supporting this motion to opposing it. Hence, the Center party prefers outcome II to outcome III.

Assumption P2:   The Conservative party and the Progress party prefer any outcome in which the farm bill amendment fails to any outcome in which it passes. Thus, they prefer outcomes II through IV to outcome I.

Office Preferences

The implications of an office-seeking model are more straightforward. I assume that Brundtland's resignation would lead to the formation of a three-party bourgeois cabinet, and that she would not resign voluntarily. Under these assumptions, the three potential coalition partners prefer office to opposition. The Progress party, which would not gain office under any circumstances, is indifferent.

Assumption O1:   The Center party and the Conservative party prefer any outcome in which the Brundtland government resigns to any outcome in which it does not. Thus, they prefer outcomes I and II to all others.

Assumption O2:   The Progress party is indifferent between outcomes in which the Brundtland government resigns and outcomes in which it does not. Thus, this party is indifferent between all outcomes.

Electoral Preferences

Finally, assume that parties are motivated strictly by future electoral success. If so, we need to look for explanations of their behavior in the anticipated electoral consequences of different strategies. Specifically, different legislative strategies may entail *individual* or *collective* electoral costs. Individual costs result from policy inconsistency, that is, from voting against party program or previous commitments. Collective electoral costs are a more complex matter. The Norwegian electorate apparently contains a significant number of sophisticated nonsocialists whose first preference is a minor party such as the Progress party or the Liberals. Yet, these voters may be induced to vote strategically for one of the three "coalitional" parties if and only if these parties jointly present a credible alternative to a Labor government. Otherwise, these individuals vote sincerely for the smaller party closest to their policy preferences.[10] In other words, these voters can be persuaded to cast a *governmental,* rather than a *partisan,* vote if they believe that a governmental choice exists. The three coalitional parties therefore have a collective electoral incentive to enhance their credibility as a potential government. Hence, they should avoid any behavior, such as overt policy disagreements, that detracts from this credibility. The Progress party, on the other hand, should for electoral purposes seek to provoke precisely such conflict.[11] Hence, the assumptions of the vote-seeking model are:

Assumption V1:   The Center party prefers any outcome in which it does not vote against its previous policy to any outcome in which it does. It also prefers voting consistently with the other coalition parties to voting contrary to one or both of them. Consequently, the Center party prefers all other outcomes to outcome III.

Assumption V2:   The Progress party prefers any outcome in which any subset of the Center party, the Christian People's party, and the Conservative party vote inconsistently with each other to any outcome in which they all vote consistently. Hence, it prefers outcome III to all others.

Assumption V3:   The Conservative party prefers voting consistently with the Center party and the Christian People's party to voting inconsistently with one or both of them. Hence, the Conservative party prefers all other outcomes to outcome III.

Table 1 summarizes the critical information about each possible outcome of the endgame. Table 2 identifies the equilibria, with the first three rows represent-

TABLE 2.   Equilibria According to Different Party Objectives

	Outcome			
Stipulated Party Objectives	I	II	III	IV
1. Office (O)	X	X	—	—
2. Policy (P)	—	X	—	X
3. Votes (V)	—	X	—	X
4. O > P	—	X	—	—
5. O > V	X	X	—	—
6. P > V	—	X	—	—
7. O > P > V	—	X	—	—

Note: X denotes a subgame perfect Nash equilibrium. Stipulations 4–7 assume lexicographic preferences.

ing the assumptions of the respective models. Three general observations can be made. First, under two of three models, there are multiple equilibria, though in neither case more than two. These multiple equilibria reflect assumptions of indifference. Second, different behavioral models yield different equilibria. Only one outcome (II) is in equilibrium under all behavioral assumptions. Third, and most tellingly, no model predicts the actual outcome (III).

Since these simple assumptions obviously do not adequately explain the Presthus debacle, we need to introduce richer and more plausible stipulations. To avoid the multiple equilibria caused by indifference, let parties be motivated by not just one, but two or all three of the objectives we have discussed. To retain as much simplicity as possible, I assume lexicographic preferences, wherein some objectives (e.g., office) dominate others (e.g., policy). In this example, policy preferences would only be decisive for outcomes between which a party is indifferent on office grounds. Stipulations (4) through (7) in table 2 represent four different models of lexicographic preferences. In each row, the party objectives, in abbreviated form, have been listed in declining order. With lexicographic preferences, the solution sets are reduced in most cases to a unique equilibrium (outcome II).

Persistent Puzzles

The problem, of course, is that outcome II failed to materialize on June 12, 1987. The Center party did *not* vote for Jan P. Syse's motion of no confidence. And if the other parties could have anticipated this move, the whole solution unravels. Three puzzles thus persist: (1) Why did the Progress party oppose the farm bill amendment, even though it turned out to be the only feasible way to give Norway the nonsocialist government the party explicitly favored? (2) Why did the Conservatives support higher farm subsidies, even though they ran counter to their program and failed to win the party either office or votes? (3) Finally, why did the Center party, after its farm bill amendment had been defeated, vote against a measure that would have put the party in government and prevented an acrimonious conflict with the other nonsocialists? The remainder of this chapter examines these questions roughly in reverse order, exploring some additional considerations that can be incorporated in an extensive-form model. These considerations include interparty differences in objectives, incomplete information, and the effects of organizational arrangements that involve party leaders in several simultaneous and interrelated games.

Complex Party Objectives

Initially, I assumed that all parties had identical goals: policy, office, or votes. I later relaxed that assumption so as to permit lexicographic preferences. Still, however, I assumed that all parties had the same objective functions. In order to grasp the June 1987 events, we need to move beyond these simplifications and to consider (1) how different goals may be traded off against each other, and (2) how parties differ in the weight they give to different objectives. Let us think of the case where political parties place positive value on all three "goods" discussed above: votes, office, and policy (see Strøm 1990a), and where trade-offs may have to be made between different goods. Table 3 defines the parameters of the endgame under the assumption that parties have objective functions that include office, policy, and votes. These parameters simply formalize objectives we have already discussed. A change of government in itself has a positive value, G, for both the Conservatives and the Center party. Passage of the farm bill amendment has a policy value, F, which is positive for the Center party but negative for the Conservatives. There is an individual electoral cost, C, of policy inconsistency and a collective cost, K, to the coalitional parties of policy disagreement. The payoff to each party is a function of these four parameters. Table 3 also includes the Progress party, which (as previously) values nonsocialist conflict positively and the farm bill amendment negatively.

TABLE 3. Parameters in Presthus Bargaining Game

Symbol	Meaning	Assumptions
G	the value of a change of government	$G_H, G_S, G_F > 0$
F	the value of an amended farm bill	$F_S > 0; F_H, F_F < 0$
C	the electoral value of policy inconsistency	$C_i < 0$ for all i
K	the electoral value of nonsocialist conflict	$K_S, K_H < 0; K_F > 0$
V	the expected value of the endgame if a farm bill amendment is rejected	—
W	the expected value of the endgame if a compromise no-confidence motion is rejected	—
$p_{H,S}$	the estimated probability of adoption of a no-confidence motion based on a farm bill amendment	$0 \leq p_{H,S} \leq 1$
$q_{H,S}$	the estimated probability of adoption of a no-confidence motion based on a policy compromise between the Center party and the Conservatives	$0 \leq q_{H,S} \leq 1$ $q_{H,S} \geq p_{H,S}$
r_F	the estimated probability of adoption of a no-confidence motion based on a policy issue chosen by the Conservatives	$0 \leq r_F \leq 1$

Note: Subscripts denoting parties represent the initials of their Norwegian names: F = Progress party, H = Conservative party, S = Center party.

I make one modification in stipulating an *instrumental* value to the Progress party of a change of government (a positive *G*). Although a nonsocialist government would yield no direct office benefits for the Progressives, it would in all probability pursue policies more favored by the party. The remaining parameters in table 3 refer to the prior bargaining game, which I shall discuss later. With this notation, we can represent the payoff structure of the endgame, as in table 4.

Intraparty Aggregation and Constraints

In order to understand the apparent irrationalities in party behavior, we now have to focus on intraparty constraints. So far, I have discussed parties as if they were unitary actors, a common simplification in the analysis of coalition politics (see Laver and Schofield 1990). In reality, parties are complex organizations of individuals with different preferences over policy, office, and votes. Organizational rules determine which of these preferences get reflected in party policy. Coalition bargaining decisions have the analytical advantage of directly involving only a small elite of leaders, as parties typically delegate such decisions to their leaders because of shortages of time and information. In such coalition negotiations, party leaders act as agents for their respective parliamentary or extraparliamentary parties (their principals). The trade-offs these leaders make between different goods, and hence the coalition agreements they are willing to accept, depend on a number of factors: (1) the feasible outcomes and payoffs, (2) the "contracts" between party leaders and their respective principals (parliamentary parties or executive committees), and (3) the private rewards to the leaders from the various outcomes.

Delegation Regimes and Party Organization

Variation in intraparty delegation regimes is a particularly interesting determinant of bargaining behavior. To prevent their leaders from strictly pursuing

TABLE 4. Payoff Matrix for Presthus Endgame

Party	Outcome			
	I	II	III	IV
Progress	$G_F + F_F + C_F$	G_F	K_F	0
Conservative	$G_H + F_H$	G_H	K_H	0
Center	$G_S + F_S$	G_S	$C_S + K_S$	0

their private rewards, parties hold them accountable through contracts and performance standards, where the ultimate sanction for poor performance is loss of office. As Luebbert observed, "party leaders are motivated above all by the desire to remain party leaders" (1986, 46), and intraparty incentives powerfully constrain their behavior in coalition bargaining. Yet, designing an effective contract for their leaders is no small matter, and parties sometimes unintentionally give their leaders incentives to behave contrary to the party interest. In the Presthus debacle, the delegation regimes of both the Center party and particularly the Conservatives ultimately backfired.

Most Norwegian parties share a similar organizational structure (see Strøm 1993). The annual (Conservatives, Progress party) or biennial (Center party) national congress (*landsmøtet*), which normally meets in the spring, is the highest formal authority within the party. Between congresses, leadership is officially exercised by two party committees elected by the congress: the national council (*landsstyret*) and the executive committee (*sentralstyret*). Norwegian parties have two top leadership positions: a chair, elected by the party congress, and a parliamentary leader elected by the party's parliamentary caucus (*stortingsgruppe*). In many parties, it is customary for a single person to hold both offices concurrently.

Despite their general similarities, the Center party, the Conservatives, and the Progress party presented somewhat different organizational features in 1987. The Conservative party traditionally had a strong parliamentary party accustomed to delegating critical decisions to its leader, whereas particularly in the Progress party the influence of the extraparliamentary leadership was stronger. More important, however, were the characteristics of the 1987 leaderships. Whereas the Center and Progress leaders were both long-term party chairs as well as parliamentary leaders, Presthus had to share power with parliamentary leader Jan P. Syse. And whereas Jakobsen and Hagen were entrenched leaders with almost ten years' tenure each, Presthus was still new and inexperienced and faced much more visible competition within his party. Internal constraints varied between the Center party and the Progress party as well. Hagen dominated his parliamentary delegation of two (himself and a military officer used to taking orders) much more effectively than Jakobsen could control his.

The Endgame: Misdelegation

Let us now return to the decisions of the three critical parties in the endgame, with an eye toward the constraints each leader faced within his own party.

The Center Party: Throwing the Steering Wheel out the Window

The most striking puzzle in the Presthus debacle is the behavior of the Center party at the last decision node, where its choices were clear. If Jakobsen rejected the censure motion from the Conservatives and the Christian People's party, his party would be left in opposition and susceptible to electoral repercussions (compare its payoffs under outcomes II and III in table 4). The farm bill amendment had already been lost. In rejecting costless office benefits and embracing electoral liabilities, the party seems deliberately to have made itself worse off.

Yet, this behavior was no accident. Immediately after Hagen's press conference, the Center party reiterated its opposition to any censure motion based on the revised national budget. The party's executive committee issued a similar proclamation the day *before* Hagen's press conference (Rommetvedt 1991, 206). At that time, Center party representatives explained their apparently uncooperative behavior as a way to force the Progress party to accept higher farm subsidies. If Hagen believed that the Center party would support a second no-confidence motion, they argued, he would have no incentive to accept higher farm spending. Game-theoretically, however, the Center party's posturing should not have been a credible threat. If ultimately forced to choose between outcomes II and III, the party would still have office as well as electoral incentives to vote *for* the no-confidence motion. Hence, Hagen could confidently call the Center party's bluff. Yet even before the final vote, neither Hagen nor the Conservative leaders apparently harbored much hope that Syse's no-confidence motion would pass. Even the Labor party taunted the Center party during the debate, essentially daring the party to bring down the government.

The key to the Center party's intransigence surely lies in intraparty constraints. Jakobsen's insistence on the farm bill amendment reflected the deep skepticism toward any Conservative coalition harbored by two MPs, Ragnhild Q. Haarstad and Lars Velsand. Haarstad and Velsand represented the so-called Hedmark guerrilla, a vocal left-wing faction of the party.[12] Jakobsen, who himself favored a change of government, appears to have precommitted himself to this group in internal party negotiations. In the parliamentary caucus on June 5, Velsand voted to accept the Labor party's farm bill. His eventual support for a censure motion was expressly conditional on the farm bill amendment. A censure motion on any other basis was unacceptable (Thomassen 1991, 33–34).[13] Haarstad was even more intransigent and proceeded to vote against her party's own (technically, Spilde's) no-confidence motion, a highly unusual occurrence in traditionally cohesive Norwegian parties.

Could Jakobsen have reneged on his commitment and thrown his weight behind the Syse no-confidence motion anyway? Jakobsen might well have faced sanctions from his parliamentary group or national executive committee in such an event. More importantly, however, a humiliating scenario might have ensued, had he supported a second no-confidence motion. The bourgeois majority in the Storting was so slender (80 to 77) that it could tolerate only one defection, such as Haarstad's on the first censure vote. Had both Haarstad and Velsand opposed Syse's no-confidence motion, it would have failed even with Progress party support, and no one would have looked more ineffectual than Jakobsen.

Thus, the Hedmark guerrilla was, in fact, pivotal, and Jakobsen may therefore have preferred the seemingly irrational strategy leading to outcome III for internal party reasons. The nested games in which the Center party leader was involved may account for his anomalous behavior (Tsebelis 1990a). His impotence was caused by the pivotal parliamentary position of the Hedmark guerrilla. This pair of parliamentarians were able to impose strict ex-ante controls on their leader's negotiations with the Conservatives. By allowing Jakobsen virtually no discretion in bargaining, the Center party had essentially "thrown the steering wheel out the window." Such brinkmanship may have helped the party in bargaining with the Conservatives, but it came back to haunt the agrarians in the parliamentary debate on June 12.

One additional consideration may have been involved in the Center party's decision. Quite possibly, Jakobsen did not think of himself as playing a one-shot game. If indeed he foresaw a series of interparty games, his concern may have been *reputation* (Calvert 1987; Kreps 1990). According to Rommetvedt (1991, 207), one Center party parliamentarian remarked in retrospect that he would have preferred a different strategy. But once the party had insisted on the farm bill amendment, it had to stick with it. In Rommetvedt's (1991, 210) words, "the party had tied itself so tightly to the mast that it could not vote for the general motion of no confidence without losing credibility at later junctures." Jakobsen thus became a victim of his own precommitment (Elster 1984).

The Conservative Party: Incompatible Incentives

As much as the Progress party won the June 1987 showdown, the Conservative party was the loser. The party failed to dislodge Brundtland, poisoned its relationship with the Center party, and suffered badly in the polls. After June 12 the political career of Rolf Presthus was effectively ruined. One could hardly imagine a less desirable outcome. Both critical Conservative decisions seem foolhardy in retrospect: acquiescence in the farm bill amendment as well as the subsequent decision to press a second no-confidence vote. Why on earth did the Conservatives go down this path to disaster?

The answer surely involves incomplete information concerning the Progress party. Presthus's dilemma also directs our attention to the internal politics of the Conservative party. The Conservatives clearly realized the risk that if the Progress party balked, their acquiescence on the farm subsidy issue would be for naught. Ideally, Presthus therefore wanted some guarantee of cooperation, either from the Progress party or from the Center party (concerning a potential second censure motion), before accepting this agenda. Unfortunately, any explicit agreement with the pariah Progress party was ruled off-limits by his two would-be coalition partners. Hence, the Conservatives repeatedly attempted to extract assurances from the Center party that the latter would remain committed to bringing down Brundtland in a potential second round.[14] Conservative parliamentary leader (and later prime minister) Jan P. Syse raised this issue on June 7. But Jakobsen steadfastly refused to issue any such guarantee.

Under this uncertainty, the prospects seem to have been estimated differently by the various Conservative leaders. Former prime minister Kåre Willoch and Storting president Jo Benkow both opposed Presthus's course of action (Bakke 1990, 187; Rommetvedt 1991, 196; Willoch 1990, 404). And though he supported Presthus, Jan P. Syse seems to have pressed more insistently for a guarantee from the Center party.[15] Did these experienced parliamentarians more correctly estimate how unlikely it was that the Progress party and the Center party would make the choices necessary to propel Presthus into the prime ministership?

Was Presthus a victim of wishful thinking? Perhaps. But according to Thomassen (1991, 35), both Presthus and Syse recognized that the farm bill amendment was a huge gamble. Presthus apparently chose to accept big risks and to "swallow camels" in order to gain the prime ministership. He was willing to accept quite unpalatable policies and take substantial electoral risks in the hope of dislodging Brundtland. Rather than any personal idiosyncrasy, however, this behavior reflected Presthus's "contract" with the Conservative party and, more specifically, the incompatibility between his incentives as an individual and the interests of the party.

After only about a year as Conservative leader, Presthus's star had already begun to fade. Though he had been elected in large part because of his perceived skills in promoting nonsocialist cooperation, he had failed to deliver the bourgeois government for which many Conservatives were hoping. A consummate insider, Presthus also had not proven to be an inspirational oppo-sition leader. The media hounded him for his failure in the "autumn hunting season" as well as for his awkward style. The party congress in Tromsø in early May 1987 made a nonsocialist government before the end of the spring session an explicit party goal, thus adding to the pressure on Presthus (Norvik 1990, 156; Thomassen 1991, 30–31; Willoch 1990, 403–4). Time was already running out for Presthus, and he knew it. The party had defined recapturing executive office as his overriding concern. Any outcome short of this goal would bode ill for Presthus's political future. On the other hand, the party had not properly defined the highest acceptable price of office.

Thus, in considering the second censure motion, Presthus may not have attached much value to the *added* electoral liability (K_H) of outcome III as compared to outcome IV. Either way, the party would remain in opposition and be electorally damaged. Presthus's leadership was also likely to come to an end. But if Presthus was thus essentially indifferent between outcomes III and IV, then any infinitesimal chance that the Center party would "tremble" and support the Syse censure motion would lead Presthus down this path (Selten 1975). In fact, the negotiators from the Conservative party and the Christian People's party took care to maximize the costs to the Center party of rejecting Syse's proposal (Rommetvedt 1991, 208).

The Conservative executive committee members may not have shared Presthus's preferences, but with customary deference they allowed him the rope by which he would come to his political demise. Presthus's gamble was approved by the party's executive committee as well as by its parliamentary caucus. In fact, in the parliamentary caucus only 3 out of 50 members were opposed (Bakke 1990, 188; Norvik 1990, 158).[16] By tradition, the Conserva-tive party's control of its leaders has taken place mainly through ex-post ac-countability. In the Norwegian Conservative party, as among tories elsewhere, nothing fails like failure, particularly in the electoral arena. Predictably, after his gamble failed, Presthus's leadership of the Conservative party was doomed. While his complicity in the design to increase farm subsidies might have been forgiven, it was much more difficult to overlook the electoral damage he had inflicted. In other words, while Presthus might have been able to trade off pol-icy goals for office with impunity, he could not get away with sacrificing the party's electorate.

Both Presthus and Jakobsen were thus constrained by their respective par-ties, but in radically different ways that reflected interesting organizational dif-ferences in delegation regimes. Jakobsen was tightly policy-constrained ex ante and in reality had no choice but to oppose Syse's censure motion. Presthus enjoyed much more policy discretion but was constrained by his ex-post office accountability to his party. He was expected to produce office benefits and knew that without results, he was eminently dispensable. Jakobsen, on the other hand, faced less obvious challenges to his leadership but was essentially powerless to make policy compromises. As we shall see later, these differences in constraints were critical to the bargaining game between the two parties.

The Bargaining Game: A War of Attrition?

Having thus explored the seemingly irrational behavior of the Center party and the Conservatives in the endgame, we now turn to their preceding bargaining game, where the assumption of full information clearly does not apply. This game was over the policy content of the no-confidence motion, for which there were three possibilities: the policy favored by the Center party (the farm bill amendment), the policy favored by the Conservatives (possibly the national budget), or some compromise. Each party had two feasible moves (or strategies): insistence or acquiescence. *Insistence* (I) means accepting only a censure motion based on the party's own preferred policy (the farm bill amendment for the Center party and the national budget for the Conservatives). *Acquiescence* (A) means accepting the other party's preferred no-confidence motion. There are four possible outcomes: mutual insistence (II), in which case no censure motion is made; mutual acquiescence (AA); Center party insistence and Conservative acquiescence (IA); or vice versa (AI).

Neither the Conservatives nor the Center party had complete information about the preferences of the Progress party, and hence they could not predict Hagen's behavior with certainty. The Progress party, on the other hand, did not have full information about the other parties' preferences. Yet we can confine the uncertainty concerning each potential censure motion to a single party: the Progress party in the cases of the farm bill amendment and the potential compromise motion, and the Center party with respect to a motion chosen by the Conservatives.

Table 3 describes three probability terms (p, q, and r) related to the likelihood of passage of the different potential censure motions. Lacking reliable information, the Center party and the Conservatives may have thought of the Progress party as having two possible types: one that would support the farm bill amendment and one that would oppose it. Absent any information to the contrary, I assume that the Center party and the Conservatives had common prior beliefs about the Progressives and use p and q to represent these prior

Conservative party (H)

	Insist (I)	Acquiesce (A)
Insist (I)	K_S, K_H	$p(G_S + F_S) + (1 - p)V_S,$ $p(G_H + F_H) + (1 - p)V_H + C_H$
Acquiesce (A)	$G_S + C_S, G_H$	$qG_S + (1 - q)W_S + C_S,$ $qG_H(1 - q)W_H + C_H$

Center party (S)

Figure 2. Strategic-form representation of Presthus bargaining game. (Subscripts denoting parties represent the initials of their Norwegian names: H = Conservative party; S = Center party. Cells are identified by row followed by column, e.g., IA.)

beliefs. The term p denotes the probability estimate of these two parties that the Progressives would support a censure motion based on a farm bill amendment (IA). Similarly, q is their (substantively less interesting) subjective probability that the Progress party would support a no-confidence motion reflecting mutual concessions by the Center party and the Conservatives (AA). Since AA could be no further from the Hagen's ideal policy than IA, q must be equal to or greater than p. For both parties, cell IA thus offers either an office bonus (with a policy outcome valued positively by the Center party and negatively by the Conservatives) with probability p, or a substantial electoral liability with probability $1 - p$. These parties' beliefs about the value of p (the Progress party's "type") must therefore have played a critical role in their decisions. Finally, r is the Progress party's probability estimate that the Center party would support a no-confidence motion based on a policy issue chosen by the Conservatives (e.g., the national budget). Table 3 contains subscripts denoting the parties whose beliefs we thus characterize. I shall in the remainder dispense with these subscripts for simplicity.

These simplifications allow us to represent the initial bargaining game in strategic form as a two-by-two matrix, shown in figure 2. The payoffs in each cell list the row player (the Center party) first and the column player (the Conservatives) second. This representation makes one important simplification: the value of the endgame in the event of a farm bill amendment censure motion is given as an unidentified expectation V. The value of V is obviously party-specific and derived from the endgame solution. Similarly, W denotes the value of an endgame following mutual acquiescence (i.e., policy concessions on both parts). (Under strategy sets II and AI there would have been no endgame.)

We can use our knowledge of the endgame to simplify these payoff functions. Assuming that Jakobsen's constraints and Presthus's incentive incom-

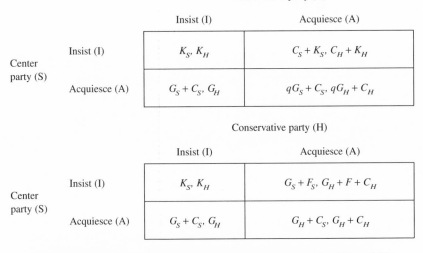

Conservative party (H)

	Insist (I)	Acquiesce (A)
Insist (I)	K_S, K_H	$C_S + K_S, C_H + K_H$
Acquiesce (A)	$G_S + C_S, G_H$	$qG_S + C_S, qG_H + C_H$

Conservative party (H)

	Insist (I)	Acquiesce (A)
Insist (I)	K_S, K_H	$G_S + F_S, G_H + F + C_H$
Acquiesce (A)	$G_S + C_S, G_H$	$G_H + C_S, G_H + C_H$

Figure 3. Bargaining game payoffs by Progress party type: (*top*) Farm bill amendment rejected ($p = 0$); (*bottom*) farm bill amendment accepted ($p = 1$). (Subscripts denoting parties represent the initials of their Norwegian names: H = Conservative party; S = Center party.)

patibilities could be foreseen, we substitute the payoffs from outcome III for V in cell IA in the payoff matrix in figure 2. For the continuation value W in cell AA, we substitute the payoffs from outcome IV of the endgame since, if Jakobsen had already acquiesced in the first round, there would have been no basis for a second censure motion. Consider next the payoffs to the Center party and the Conservatives if the Progress party's type had been known. Figure 3 illustrates the two possibilities by setting p equal to 0 and 1, respectively. With $p = 0$, and assuming $K \geq C$ and $0 < q < 1$, both parties have the same preference ordering over the four outcomes: AI > AA > II > IA. Note that the actual outcome is the *worst possible* result for *both* parties. In this game, both parties have dominant strategies. The Center party will acquiesce and the Conservatives insist. If, on the other hand, $p = 1$ and $q = 1$, then the Center party has the following preference ordering: IA > AA, AI > II, and the Conservatives: AI > AA > IA > II. This is essentially a game of *Chicken*.[17]

But the one-shot, simultaneous-move nature of Chicken is not the best representation of the bargaining game between the Center party and the Conservatives. Since their bargaining proceeded over a considerable period, the *war of attrition* is a more accurate model. The war of attrition is essentially Chicken "stretched out over time." Each player can in each time period choose to stay ("insist") or exit ("acquiesce"). The last player to stay earns a reward, but until all but one exit, all who stay pay a penalty in each period (Fudenberg and Tirole 1991, 119–26; Rasmusen 1989, 74–75). A continuous-time version of this game also has the advantage of effectively eliminating the implausible outcome AA, that is, both parties acquiescing simultaneously.

Chicken has two equilibria in pure strategies: IA and AI. In the two-player Chicken or war of attrition, II (mutual insistence or intransigence) is the worst outcome for each player, and in any pure-strategy equilibrium one player insists and the other acquiesces. The game itself, however, does not provide much of a clue as to which player will acquiesce ("swerve"). And if the players can adopt mixed strategies, the dominated strategy set AA occurs with regularity (Rasmusen 1989, 74). The war of attrition also has mixed-strategy equilibria in which each player exits (acquiesces) with a constant probability at each move as long as his opponent has not already done so. Contrary to the regular war of attrition, however, in the Presthus bargaining game the penalty for mutual intransigence rose dramatically toward the end of the parliamentary session, when the opposition parties suddenly would have to wait four months and go through local elections before they would have another shot at the government. As the end of the session approached, the incentives to acquiesce therefore increased dramatically. No surprise, therefore, that the Center party and the Conservatives reached agreement on a censure motion only two days before the summer recess.

Why Presthus Blinked

The Center party took a tough bargaining stance vis-à-vis the Conservatives. Its precommitment to intransigence is a time-honored strategy in Chicken and the war of attrition. If one player can find a way to move first (e.g., through credible precommitment), then he can safely insist, knowing that the second player, on observing this behavior, can do no better than to acquiesce. The fact that the Center party (and less successfully, perhaps, the Conservatives) so clearly adopted this strategy suggests a belief that p was significantly larger than zero. Yet, credible precommitments in Chicken are difficult to make, and they can be disastrous if they fail to deter (Taylor 1987, 45–49). Every player has an incentive to bluster, and credible commitments may require dramatic measures ("throwing the steering wheel out the window"). While Jakobsen's tough stance probably helped the Center party prevail in the bargaining game, it did not deter the Conservatives from embarrassing him with a second censure motion in the endgame.

What other factors might account for the Center party's success against the Conservatives in the bargaining game? Two factors suggest themselves: (1) the credible policy constraints on Jakobsen versus the wide discretion given to Presthus, and (2) the greater impatience (higher discount rate) of Presthus, due again to his personal incentives. The resistance Jakobsen faced from the Hedmark guerrilla helped make his threats credible. Conservative leaders presumably knew of this opposition, as it was in the Center party leader's interest to inform them that his hands were tied. Presthus's greater impatience contributed to the same outcome. In the war of attrition, players' ability to hold out generally depend on their discount rates. All else equal, the player with the higher discount rate, that is, the more impatient one, is more likely to acquiesce early. The Conservative party congress in May had done Presthus a disservice by publicly requesting a coalition before the parliamentary recess. Center party negotiators knew that Presthus had the latitude to make policy compromises, and that he needed a quick fix. These circumstances eventually doomed the Conservatives in their negotiations.

The Progress Party: The Value of Private Information

Clearly, the Progress party was the greatest unknown factor in the Presthus debacle. Guesses about the preferences of the Progress party were therefore critical to the calculations of the other parties. The private information the Progress party had about its own type can be a source of considerable power. Carl I. Hagen exploited this advantage to the hilt, playing his cards extremely close to his chest. The public statements Hagen made prior to his dramatic press conference on June 11 were studiedly ambiguous. When it became increasingly clear that the farm bill would be the basis of the no-confidence motion, Hagen tempered his enthusiasm about the bourgeois coalition. On June 6 he admitted to doubts about the three-party coalition, citing internal differences and the lack of a clear policy alternative to the Labor government (Rommetvedt 1991, 196). Two days later he reiterated his opposition to increased agricultural transfers, yet the following day he told journalists that his party might well vote against the government's farm bill anyway.

In his equivocation, Hagen kept stressing the need to consult his party's national and regional officers, many of whom were known to oppose any policy compromise. And in Hagen's public justification of his final decision, the voice of his party's activists had a prominent place. Were Hagen's hands then tied by his organization, due, perhaps, to his party's commitment to reducing transfers to Norwegian agriculture? Not likely. Hagen's personal authority in his party was immense, and on a similar issue in 1985 he had, without serious repercussions, voted against his party's program in order to save Willoch. Hagen's deference to his party's officers was therefore probably more of a rationalization than a rationale.

What was fundamentally at stake for the Progress party? Consider table 4, which shows the endgame payoff matrix. Assuming that Hagen correctly anticipated the eventual result of opposing Spilde's censure motion (outcome III), then the Progress party's decision hinged on the magnitude of its benefit from nonsocialist conflict relative to the three other terms. Specifically, the party should vote for the censure motion if the net benefit of a change of government, minus the cost of an amended farm bill, minus the electoral cost of voting contrary to its program, exceeded the party's electoral rewards from conflict between the other nonsocialist parties. Hagen's strategy, then, would be to vote yes if and only if:

$$G_F + F_F + C_F \geq K_F$$

Before June 11, presumably no one outside the Progress party knew whether this condition held. But although the Progress party kept Norwegians in suspense about its intentions, one thing was perfectly clear. If the government's farm bill and the no-confidence motion were separated, the Progressives would support both and thereby give the country a bourgeois cabinet without higher agricultural spending. Hagen had committed his party as early as May 29 by declaring that the Progress party would support a Conservative censure motion (AI) (Rommetvedt 1991, 191). As it turned out, Hagen would not have the luxury of separating these two issues. Until June 11, however, he remained noncommittal concerning the farm bill amendment (IA) favored by the Center party.

In all likelihood, Hagen's precommitment to no confidence on the revised national budget was designed to strengthen the Conservatives in their negotiations with the Center party. If the Conservatives could prevail in their bargaining, then the Progressives would have their most preferred outcome. But why did Hagen not further boost the bargaining power of the Conservatives by fully revealing his type, that is, by clearly rejecting a farm bill amendment? The Progress party, after all, had both electoral and policy incentives to vote against Spilde's censure motion. One possibility is that the Center party might not have believed such a threat. After all, Hagen had an incentive to engage in cheap talk of this kind regardless of his actual intentions.

But equivocation may in fact have been Hagen's best strategy. At first glance, this seems incompatible with the claim that a no-confidence vote based on the Conservatives' policy choice would have been the Progress party's most preferred outcome. But Hagen may not have been convinced that if he revealed his type, the Conservative censure motion would in fact pass. That outcome would hinge on whether the Center party leadership could convince at least one of the two Hedmark guerrillas to go along. Assume that Hagen attached a probability of r to this outcome. Alternatively, if Hagen had revealed his private information and the requisite Center party support had not been forthcoming, the result would essentially have been a null event. The Center party and the Conservatives would both have had an incentive to paper over their differences, no censure motion would have been made, and no policy would have been affected. I therefore attribute a subjective probability of $1 - r$ and a zero value to this outcome for the Progress party. The Progress party should rationally only reveal its type if $rG_F \geq K_F$, that is, if the value of a nonsocialist government, times the probability that the Center party would bring it about, at least outweighed the electoral benefit the Progressives could draw from a coalitional debacle. If Hagen's estimate of r was low, then he had an incentive to deliberately mislead the coalitional parties down the garden path.

Hagen's electoral considerations (K_F versus C_F) were in themselves probably something of a lottery. If he accepted increased farm subsidies, he stood to suffer a predictable loss of votes among his libertarian supporters. A poll published on June 11 showed little popular support for the farm bill amendment. Only 11.7 percent of the voters thought this was an appropriate issue on which to defeat the government, and even among nonsocialists, two-thirds considered this a contrived way to generate a cabinet crisis (Rommetvedt 1991, 205). If, on the other hand, Hagen made the much more dramatic gesture of opposing the bourgeois no-confidence motion, the electoral fallout would be much more unpredictable. In a similar situation in 1963, when the Socialist People's party brought down Einar Gerhardsen's Labor government, it suffered stinging losses among voters incensed at its complicity in the formation of Norway's first postwar bourgeois government. Hagen, however, gambled on his ability to frame the issues in such a way that he would appear the principled and responsible statesman rather than the traitor to the nonsocialist cause. Given the party's precarious electoral position, the Progressives could ill afford even a small, but certain, electoral setback. Even a drop of 0.5 percent in the national poll could have deprived the party of its parliamentary representation. Better, then, to gamble at the high-stakes tables. His party's weakness among the voters made Hagen highly risk-acceptant over electoral outcomes, and willing to take his case to the people. In this endeavor, he was amazingly successful, probably beyond his wildest imagination.

Conclusion

I have examined a spectacular case of coalition bargaining failure in recent Norwegian history. The Presthus debacle of 1987 is not easily accounted for by traditional explanations based on cooperative coalition theory. Through an alternative extensive-form game model, I have analyzed the ill-fated strategies of the protagonists and teased out their motivations. This mode of analysis allows us to consider the implications of asymmetric information, variations in objective functions, structured vs. unstructured bargaining environments, the sequence of bargaining, time preferences, and internal delegation regimes in political parties.

Whereas Hagen was seeking electoral gains and Jakobsen farm subsidies, Presthus was primarily concerned with office payoffs. These differences in party behavior were in large part a function of intraparty politics. The Presthus case offers us no happy medium between the Scylla of strict ex-ante policy constraint (Jakobsen) and the Charybdis of ex-post office accountability (Presthus). Both the Conservatives and the Center party featured delegation regimes ill-suited to the bargaining situation in which they found themselves, and much of the responsibility for the Presthus debacle rests with these internal structures of Norwegian political parties. The lack of similar constraints in the Progress party made it possible for Hagen to place greater weight on electoral objectives and to take substantial risks. Hagen's humiliation of Jakobsen and especially Presthus demonstrates the value of private information. His control over private information enabled him to entice the coalitional parties into behavior that was ultimately self-destructive. And Jakobsen's tough bargaining stance highlights the attractions and perils of precommitment.

Even without misdelegation or deliberate manipulation, however, the bargaining situation faced by Presthus and his associates invited disaster. The game of Chicken (played with mixed strategies) occasionally produces outcomes that are catastrophic for everybody. The war of attrition, which the Presthus debacle even more closely resembles, can have similarly unpleasant results. Moreover, misperception and bargaining failure were particularly likely in the Presthus debacle due to the impending summer recess. The closer the end of the session drew, the higher the stakes, until the flurry of frenzied activity in the last few days before the guillotine fell. Such frantic times have a way of producing ill-considered behavior, a phenomenon well known from congressional budget debates in the United States (Cox and Kernell 1991).

Thus, the calendar, information, and structure are important keys to the dismal fate of Rolf Presthus and his would-be coalition partners. Given time, knowledge, and appropriate incentives, the story might have been a happier one for Presthus, Jakobsen, and Bondevik (and less triumphant for Hagen and Brundtland). And though, sadly, the main protagonist cannot now benefit from this knowledge, the student of coalition behavior can. Bargaining failures can offer us valuable insight into party behavior, and noncooperative game theory affords us useful tools with which to explain the dramas that elite-level politics occasionally produces.

NOTES

1. The 1965–71 cabinet, headed by Per Borten of the Center party, was a four-party coalition, whereas the 1983–86 government failed to include the Liberals (Venstre). The Liberals lost their parliamentary representation in 1985 and were therefore not a relevant party in the events described here.

2. I use the terms *nonsocialist* and *bourgeois* interchangeably. This usage is consistent with Norwegian convention and is neither derogatory nor indicative of a class-analytic perspective. In fact, the nonsocialist parties frequently apply the label *bourgeois* (*borgerlig*) to themselves.

3. One member of the Center party, Ragnhild Queseth Haarstad, voted against her party's position on this bill. After disposing of Spilde's no-confidence motion, the Storting overwhelmingly, by a vote of 123 to 34, rejected a motion by Arent Henriksen of the Socialist Left party to increase agricultural appropriations.

4. Here as elsewhere, I am responsible for all translations from the Norwegian.

5. It might seem that one or more additional no-confidence motions could follow end node III. As the following argument shows, however, outcome III implies that no such motion would pass. Since I assume that the coalitional parties bear an electoral cost if they propose divisive no-confidence motions, we can disregard any further agenda.

6. Perfect information implies that each player knows (1) who the other players are, (2) the set of actions available to each player, (3) all potential payoffs to each player, and (4) all previous moves. Certainty means that the outcome is not affected by random, unpredictable events ("moves by Nature") that take place after the players have made their choices (Rasmusen 1989, 51).

7. A Nash equilibrium is a set of strategies from which no player has an incentive to deviate as long as no other player does. In other words, no player can make himself better off by unilaterally changing his strategy. The Nash equilibria identified in figure 1 are subgame perfect because they satisfy the requirements of backward induction. On subgame perfection, see Selten 1975 and Rasmusen 1989. I also assume here that all players adopt pure strategies, i.e., that no player's strategy is a lottery over several feasible moves. This assumption seems both plausible and parsimonious here.

8. All preference relations are strict unless otherwise indicated.

9. This does not imply that the Center party or the Conservatives prefer voting

for their respective programs to not voting. Hence, the Conservatives have no *policy* incentive to introduce the Syse motion.

10. Such voters may base their decisions on preferences over final policies rather than preferences over parties (or candidates) per se. Austen-Smith and Banks (1988) argue that policy preferences are the more theoretically satisfactory assumption in models of multiparty competition and use this stipulation to generate strong analytical results.

11. This interpretation is corroborated by the 1987 events. Polls taken immediately after the Presthus debacle showed marked declines for the Conservatives (from 30.2 to 27.1 percent) as well as the Center party (from 5.9 to 5.2 percent). The Christian People's party, which had been conciliatory throughout, registered a modest gain (8.1 to 8.4 percent). But the big winner was the Progress party, which leapt from 5.1 to 7.1 percent (Rommetvedt 1987). These figures represent the means of polls by several authoritative firms. The pre-event poll figures are the averages of polls by Norsk Gallup, Markeds- og Mediainstituttet (MMI), and Scan Fact. The postevent figures represent the means of polls by Norsk Gallup and Opinion. See Rommetvedt 1987 for details. The Progress party later continued to surge, reaching a stunning 12.3 percent of the national vote in the September regional elections, more than twice its poll in any previous election.

12. This unofficial faction takes its name from the province of Hedmark, an agricultural area in east central Norway and the constituency of Ragnhild Q. Haarstad. The province is a traditional stronghold of the Center party.

13. In his memoirs, Petter Thomassen (1991, 33) reports that the internal debate in the Center party was so intense that Jakobsen wept when Velsand came around to supporting the farm bill amendment. Thomassen is a leading Conservative who served as minister of industry in one of the Willoch cabinets (1985–86).

14. Bente Bakke, a maverick Conservative backbencher, reports that the need for a precommitment from the other coalitional parties was strongly felt within the Conservative parliamentary caucus. After the failed "autumn hunting season" the previous year, parliamentary leader Jan P. Syse had reportedly assured the members that no further assaults on the Brundtland government would be attempted without the binding agreement of both the Christian People's party and the Center party (Bakke 1990, 179–86).

15. Jan P. Syse later replaced Presthus as chair of the Conservative party. In October 1989 he became prime minister in charge of the same three-party coalition that Presthus had tried to establish. Syse's coalition, which was fragile from the very beginning, broke down after only one year in office.

16. The three skeptics were a prestigious group, however. They included Willoch, Benkow, and one backbencher.

17. The payoff structure in this game would have been true Chicken had the Center party strictly preferred AA to AI. The party's indifference between these two outcomes makes no difference to the game's equilibrium, however.

Chapter 2

Why Do Trade Unions Call Strikes That Seem Sure to Fail?

Miriam A. Golden

Across the advanced capitalist countries millions of people have lost their jobs in recent decades. Why have trade unions at times appeared indifferent even as thousands of their members have been thrown out of work whereas on other occasions they have undertaken lengthy and bitter strikes when threatened with only temporary layoffs?

This chapter demonstrates that unemployment carries with it substantially different effects for trade unions and firms—and ultimately for governments and citizens—depending on the institutional mechanisms used to allocate job loss. Work in microeconomics identifies institutional conditions under which unions are or are not indifferent to the level of employment chosen by the firm. I extend this line of analysis to delineate the conditions under which trade unions acquiesce to mass work-force reductions rather than resorting to industrial action. These different outcomes, I argue, result from calculations union officials make regarding the effects of institutional features of the labor market: namely, the presence or absence of seniority-based selection mechanisms for allocating layoffs. It follows that the often highly emotive rhetoric that typically invests strikes that occur in the face of mass work-force reductions is misleading. Rather than trying to prevent job loss, such strikes seek to establish selection criteria for dismissal or layoff.[1] I illustrate this argument empirically with analyses of industrial disputes at the Italian Fiat works in 1980 and at British Leyland (BL; subsequently Austin Rover) between 1979 and 1980.

This chapter proceeds as follows: first, I lay out the analytic problem. I then discuss the research design and the criteria used for case selection. Following that, I present empirical materials from two cases. I then examine some interpretations from the literature. Finally, I offer an alternative hypothesis drawn from rational choice and assess the empirical evidence against it.

Statement of the Problem

Let us imagine that management informs organized labor that it intends to reduce the number of its employees by at least 10 percent, which I take as a convenient threshold for mass work-force reductions. In this interaction, capital takes the initiative with its announcement of job cuts; if we were to characterize the situation as a game, we would say that capital moved first.[2]

Although forced to respond to management's initiatives, choice nonetheless remains open to organized labor. In answering the threat of work-force reductions, labor can either acquiesce or resist. It can grumble, protest, and then effectively accede; or it can undertake major industrial action. The explanatory task of what follows is to specify why organized labor, confronted with equally intransigent representatives of capital, sometimes acquiesces and sometimes resists.

The question is of interest for at least three reasons. First, resistance, when it occurs, typically entails a lengthy, expensive, and politically important dispute. Particularly in an era of high unemployment, when workers generally hesitate to undertake industrial action, the sheer drama of such a strike elicits curiosity.

Second, union responses to mass work-force reductions shed light on the nature of union power in market economies. Although unable to prevent job loss itself from occurring, unions do often influence the criteria according to which particular workers are selected for redundancy (permanent dismissal) or layoff. Unions thereby enact different principles of justice, playing a normative role in the workings of the market (see Elster 1992).

Finally, the empirical puzzle of union responses to job loss is not well captured by existing theories of political economy. There is a substantial literature delineating the conditions under which labor relations in advanced capitalism prove cooperative. In the economically turbulent years that we date from the first oil shock of 1973–74, good labor relations have been identified as a possibly important component of superior economic performance (Cameron 1984; Katzenstein 1985; Lange and Garrett 1985). Stress has been laid on how the structures of organized labor promote good labor relations nationally. By this account, the fragmented and decentralized union movements found in Britain, the United States, France, and Italy are seen as handicapping corporatist quiescence, associated instead with the unified and highly centralized union movements of Central Europe and Scandinavia (Cameron 1984; Korpi and Shalev 1980).[3]

Similar conclusions emerge from studies of firm restructuring and reorganization. Typically working (if only by implication) from a similar macrolevel framework, industrial relations specialists, particularly those concerned with the automobile industry—the sector to have elicited the bulk of relevant research in recent years—have identified a cluster of microlevel variables that they believe are associated with cooperative labor relations in the firm. Like their macrolevel counterparts, such studies are attentive to the importance of union attributes. For instance, a cross-national study of restructuring in the automobile industry carried out in the early 1980s echoes the corporatist literature when noting that noncooperative "resistance to change should be strongest in systems that combine competitive multiunionism with 'sectional' shop-floor autonomy and effective challenges to management's 'right to manage'" (Altshuler et al. 1984, 214; see also Streeck and Hoff 1983, 28–36). Various studies have identified France, Italy, and Britain as especially unlikely to generate cooperative trade unionism (Altshuler et al. 1984, 211; Streeck and Hoff 1983).

The corporatist and the industrial relations literatures thus class Italy and Britain together for similar reasons: in both countries, histories of multiple, competitive unionism in conjunction with strong shop-floor movements are seen as incapable of promoting cooperative industrial relations, whether nationally (corporatism) or in the firm (during restructuring). Surprisingly, however, when it came to restructuring the automobile industry, British and Italian industrial relations were characterized by different, not similar, outcomes. Whereas organized labor at British Leyland acceded to mass work-force reductions, its Italian counterpart resisted.

While comparative political economy has not done a good job in explaining these different outcomes, I propose a theory that is able to explain these apparently anomalous results. Rather than view British and Italian industrial relations systems as historical artifacts best understood with reference to national traditions and organizational attributes of unions, I suggest that we look to those who decide union responses to work-force reductions, namely, union officials. I propose that we analyze them as if they were rational, calculating agents principally concerned with protecting their own organizations. I argue that their assessments of how best to do so are functions of relatively simple features of the labor market institutions regulating manpower, namely, seniority systems. In short, I propose an ahistorical, microlevel account of union behavior, one focused on the choices union officials make within the institutional constraints of the firm.

Research Design and Case Selection

Trade union responses to job loss have not received much systematic inquiry, although the issue has figured as one of incidental importance in comparative analyses of industrial restructuring (e.g., Rhodes and Wright 1988). I deploy a similar systems research design, in which cases are matched along potentially important dimensions but differ in their outcomes on the dependent variable, thereby permitting systematic evaluation of various hypotheses. Rival hypotheses can be assessed according to whether the independent variables proposed exhibit variation appropriate to the observed outcomes. I show that, for the two cases investigated, the presence or absence of a seniority device varies with union acquiescence or resistance to job loss; at the same time, I show that a number of other factors—including the ideological preferences of shop stewards, the relative influence of stewards within organized labor, the extent of union fragmentation and decentralization, the credibility of management's threat, and the potential impact of job loss on workers—did not vary for the two cases. Given their different outcomes, I argue that this rules out these variables as plausible explanatory factors. Finally, I show that the outcome associated with one of the two cases was reversed when its standing on the seniority issue had been reversed in the past.

The two cases I investigate were selected on the basis of their genuine empirical importance as well for the similarities exhibited in their preexisting conditions. The sheer empirical importance of the two cases is indisputable. Industrial relations at British Leyland are often taken as indicative of British manufacturing more generally (Willman and Winch 1985, 188). For Italy, Fiat has been historically viewed in the same light. Indeed, these two firms are virtually synonymous with their national automobile industries,[4] making company and sectoral analysis almost indistinguishable. Given the sheer size of the automobile industry as well as the national and even international publicity that events in these firms receive, outcomes here carry an importance that far exceeds that usually characterizing single firms.

Events in both cases took place almost simultaneously, following on the heels of the second oil shock. Conditions at British Leyland and Fiat were at that time remarkably similar. In both firms, newly appointed and aggressively antilabor managing directors or chairmen announced massive job reductions as part of more general plans for firm restructuring and reorganization (Edwardes 1983; Romiti 1988). Both firms had been suffering poor productivity and losing market share to foreign competitors. In both cases, too, poor productivity was viewed by management as a function of overmanning; overmanning, in turn, was seen as an outcome of poor industrial relations. Union organizations at British Leyland and at Fiat enjoyed reputations as highly militant and strike-prone, with strongly entrenched shop steward organizations in whose leadership organs Communist party members figured prominently.

Given these similar conditions, management's decision to tackle overmanning became invested with similar significance. One study has summarized the major issue involved in both cases as the "re-establishment of managerial authority," including the very authority to effect work-force reductions. Comparing the outcomes at British Leyland and Fiat, Streeck (1985, 21) notes that "the more or less complete recovery of the two companies by the mid-1980s is accounted for mainly by the fact that management prevailed on this crucial, and cruel subject." Both firms were intransigently committed to effecting massive work-force reductions.

Finally, the situations facing employees were similar in both firms. Fiat and British Leyland are centered in monoindustrial regions whose occupational structures are dominated by the automobile industry. Job loss was thus especially threatening to employees, since work in other local industries was unlikely to be easily found. Mass work-force reductions in the automobile industry were also likely to carry with them considerable secondary unemployment, as the effects rippled through the local economies (see Golden 1988, 192–95; Walker 1987). In both cases, however, the threat to autoworkers was more of temporary layoff or voluntary severance than of forced redundancy, and work-force reductions were achieved with the nearly total protection of employees' incomes (on BL, see Taylor 1981, 70; on Fiat, see below).

Two Cases of Job Loss

Notwithstanding these similar conditions, in one case organized labor acquiesced to job loss whereas in the other a long and bitter strike ensued. Shop stewards at British Leyland attempted to muster mass resistance to proposed work-force reductions in 1979. Failing to gain the support of the national unions involved, they gave in to the company's plan to shed nearly 30 percent of its work force. Less than a year later, shop stewards at the Italian Fiat works successfully rallied their national leaders behind a thirty-five-day strike over a proposed work-force reduction of only 17 percent of those employed by the company's automobile division in Italy (calculated using figures reported in

Comito 1982, appendix, table 5). They lost the strike, and over the next three years employment in Fiat's automobile plants in Italy fell by a third. The next section provides details of these two sets of events.

The Fiat Strike of 1980

In early May 1980, Italy's largest private employer, Fiat, S.p.A. announced that it was experiencing profitability and productivity problems so severe that it was going to put 78,000 autoworkers on reduced work hours.[5] (Italian law provides for reduced work hours, as well as temporary layoff, through the *cassa integrazione guadagni* [CIG], which guarantees some 90 percent of an employee's wage [in English, see Treu 1982].) By June, under pressure from its creditors, the company was threatening mass firings, a phenomenon unknown in large Italian industry for over a decade. In order to make its threat fully credible, Fiat replaced its managing director with one notorious· for his hawkish views on industrial relations. Meanwhile, the company continued to declare both publicly and in private discussions with the three trade unions representing its employees—which together comprised the Federazione Lavoratori Metalmeccanici (FLM), the joint industrial union organizing Italy's engineering and metalworking industries—that it intended to fire large numbers of autoworkers. After months of fruitless negotiations over the fate of what had by now become 24,000 employees to be temporarily laid off, in September Fiat sent out letters permanently dismissing some 13,000 Turinese autoworkers and another 1,300 steelworkers as of early October (the company is based in Turin, where most of its plants are located). A bitter strike ensued, becoming a national political issue. The general secretary of Italy's Communist party spoke outside Fiat's gates, for instance, promising that if employees occupied the factory, the party would be in there with them.

In late September, the Italian government fell. In view of this, the company rescinded the threat to fire, at least until the end of the year, and instead temporarily laid off 24,000 employees for three months. Paradoxically, this appeared only to inflame the unions organizing industrial action. Tactics hardened, Fiat plants were blockaded, and, in an extremely unusual move, 24-hour picket lines were set up. Since Italian unions maintain no strike funds, industrial action there usually involves short, revolving events, not walkouts. All-out strikes are almost impossible to sustain, since employees encounter severe financial hardships virtually immediately; thus, the temptation to strike-break is very strong.

The strike ended only when 40,000 Fiat workers (mainly but not exclusively skilled workers, foremen, and white-collar staff) took to the streets of Turin in a public procession demanding the "right to work" (Baldissera 1984). It was the first mass display of anti-union sentiment in Italy in decades, and it subsequently engendered the formation of a new and rival trade union organizing white-collar staff.

An agreement (Federazione CGIL-CISL-UIL Piemonte 1980, XXV–XXVII) was signed thirty-five days after the strike had begun. It specified that no workers were to be fired, although 23,000 were to be temporarily laid-off for up to three years. Nonetheless, the strike was a public relations debacle for organized labor, the most crushing in twenty-five years. The unions lost the main demand put forth during the strike itself: essentially, work-sharing in place of layoffs. They had asked that work-force reductions take place through a combination of natural wastage, early retirement schemes, and rotating layoffs among employees. Although the company promised that no redundancies would occur and that work-force reductions would be effected using nominally temporary layoffs, management refused to rotate layoffs.

The Reorganization of British Leyland between 1979 and 1981

Prior to 1979, the situation at British Leyland, Britain's nationalized automobile producer, was similar to that at Fiat.[6] In both firms, industrial relations were identified as the main factor damaging productivity (on the United Kingdom, see Jones and Prais 1978). Observers focused on the impact of the job controls exercised by shop steward organizations. Following the second oil shock, both firms faced severe financial losses that their boards of directors decided to handle with substantial cutbacks in personnel in conjunction with systematic attempts at regaining authority on the shop floor. In other words, shop stewards were to be deprived of much of their influence, and job controls were to be attenuated if not eradicated.

British Leyland began cutting jobs in 1978, but restructuring only really got under way the following year. In June 1979, the company's managing director, Michael (later Sir Michael) Edwardes, announced a Recovery Plan involving thirteen plant closures and personnel reductions of some 25,000. Shop stewards voted immediately to oppose the plan. The executive of the Confederation of Shipbuilding and Engineering Unions (CSEU), a peak association (see Seglow and Wallace 1984, 10; Willman and Winch 1985, 112), supported the Recovery Plan, recommending to employees that they accept it.

The company balloted the work force on the Recovery Plan in October. Employees turned out to vote by a rate of four to one; voters approved the Plan by 87 percent (Willman and Winch 1985, 185, table 9, 1). Edwardes then produced a ninety-two-page "Draft Agreement" detailing the changes in working practices sought by the company. It proposed an end to what was known as "mutuality"—namely, agreements that gave shop stewards rights to negotiate virtually all matters of work effort, job performance, and demarcations.

In November, despite the rank and file's evident support for the Recovery Plan, the senior shop steward at the company's Longbridge facility—a man the popular press called "the most powerful shop steward in British industry" (*Sunday Times* [London], November 25, 1979, 63)—took on the Recovery Plan with a pamphlet exhorting workers to resist reorganization and in particular to mobilize against plant closures and job loss even with "work-ins and occupations" if necessary (Leyland Combine Trade Union Committee n.d., 13). The company responded by sacking the steward.

The Transport and General Workers' Union (TGWU), both Britain's and British Leyland's largest union, called for industrial action to protest the sacking. But the steward's own union, the Amalgamated Union of Engineering Workers (AUEW), waffled. Although the AUEW formally supported its steward, launching an inquiry into his dismissal (Wilks 1984, 211), some have suggested that the AUEW may have tacitly endorsed the company's Draft Agreement and the diminution in steward power it entailed (see Scarbrough 1982, II, 82; also Jefferys 1988, 79–80). Edwardes himself apparently found the AUEW more cooperative than the TGWU (Edwardes 1983). With the two major unions at Longbridge divided, strike action protesting the dismissal fizzled.

In April, having failed to gain employee agreement to the ninety-two-page document on new pay and working practices, the company issued what was commonly called the "Blue Newspaper," a shortened "Final Draft of Proposed Agreement on Bargaining, Pay, Employee Benefits and Productivity" (BL Cars 1980) aimed at the manual work force. Management announced that anyone reporting to work on April 8 would be considered to have accepted the changes. Anyone staying away was simply to be fired. The end of mutuality was thereby unilaterally imposed, and new working practices speedily implemented (Willman 1984, 9). The company's work force in the United Kingdom was halved between 1978 and 1982 (Centre for Policy Studies 1983, 31, table 12).

Five Empirical Hypotheses

Management at Fiat and British Leyland launched similar attacks on organized labor at the end of the 1970s. But the responses of their union movements differed. At Fiat, organized labor—from the lowest shop steward to the highest confederal officer—resisted job loss with a long and bitter strike. At British Leyland, conversely, attempts to muster resistance by shop stewards faltered in the face of determined opposition by national union officials, who ensured labor's acquiescence to job loss and restructuring. I now consider five arguments from the case-specific analyses that have grown up around the two sets of events described. Each is deficient, I show, when we extend it to the other case included here. Hence, none of the five possible explanations is persuasive for both sets of events.

1. *The radical shop steward argument:*   The most systematic study of the Fiat strike (Bonazzi 1984; Carmignani 1984) argues that it was the company's highly ideological steward organization that engendered militant resistance to job loss—a steward organization that vetoed less radical proposals from above (Bonazzi 1984), despite a relatively moderate rank and file which tended to acknowledge that the firm was effectively overmanned (Bonazzi 1988, 5). The incentive for stewards to engage in radical ideological position-taking came, according to this view, as an attempt to compensate for their cooptation into shop-floor decision making and their roles as agents of social control vis-à-vis the rest of the work force (Bonazzi 1987).

Shop stewards at British Leyland had also become involved in shop-floor social control (see Scarbrough 1986, 109–10; Willman and Winch 1985, 83), and they too engaged in ideological position-taking of a kind more or less identical to that of their Italian colleagues. Perhaps not surprisingly, both groups reacted similarly to the threat of work-force reductions, expressing preferences for militant resistance to job loss, resistance extending even to threats of factory occupations. But in one case national union leaders repudiated the stewards, whereas in the other they supported their claims. An explanation that is exclusively focused on shop stewards is inadequate for understanding why different outcomes resulted.

2. *The powerful shop steward argument:*   If the preferences of stewards at Fiat and British Leyland were indistinguishable, perhaps stewards in Italy enjoyed greater autonomy and influence than stewards in Britain; that is, perhaps in cases of disagreement between national officials and stewards, stewards in Italy are either capable of independent action or able to force national officials to act according to the preferences of the stewards.

If anything, the empirical evidence suggests that it is British, not Italian, stewards who enjoy greater autonomy and discretion (for Britain, I draw on Batstone, Boraston, and Frenkel 1977 and Clegg 1979, chap. 2 and 213–21; for

Italy, on Golden 1988, 103–10). Relations between stewards and union officials have historically been more tense in Britain than in Italy, and the British steward system often developed in opposition to national trade unionism. In collective bargaining, British stewards generally enjoy greater freedom from union supervision and control from above.

Differences in steward autonomy and influence are not, however, enough to explain the different outcomes that characterize the two cases. In Italy as much as in Britain, national unions chose whether to endorse or repudiate steward action. Their decisions did not necessarily coincide with the preferences of shop stewards or with the apparent degree of steward autonomy and influence. While it is true that stewards supplied the crucial impulse behind the Fiat strike, they did so *only because national officials allowed them to*. Nothing in the constitution of Italian unionism prevented national officials from repudiating their stewards, thereby suffocating strike action, as their British counterparts did. In the British case union officials (especially in the AUEW) refused to back a strike[7] although it was supported by an ostensibly more powerful steward movement, whereas in the Italian case national union leaders supported industrial action. This suggests that they viewed it as in their own interests to do so.

3. *The union structure argument:*   Perhaps if authority relations within the two union movements were fundamentally similar, outcomes would have been different had the structures of organized labor differed. This view has been advanced by those who argue that at British Leyland "the plant-based and sectionalized union structure was too decentralized to provide a cohesive defense of their members' interests in the crises of the late 1970s" (Marsden et al. 1985, 140), suggesting that resistance would have occurred had organized labor only been less fragmented and more centralized. Events at Fiat reveal that this attention to structure is misplaced. At Fiat a union movement in many ways equally fragmented and decentralized nonetheless mustered a "cohesive defense." It did so because, despite the handicaps of structure, national union officials backed shop stewards in their determination to resist layoffs.

4. *The management credibility argument:*   Perhaps British Leyland's management successfully convinced British national union officials that it was not bluffing in its threats to close the firm entirely if labor tried to repudiate the Recovery Plan with a long strike, whereas Fiat's failed to convince Italian union officials that a last-minute rescue operation (funded by the government) wouldn't be forthcoming rather than allow the firm to declare bankruptcy. Evidence for this comes from British Leyland's own management, which subsequently stressed the importance it had placed on convincing national union officials as well as the rank and file that the government was no longer prepared

to bail out the company with funds except under conditions of severe demanning and restructuring (Edwardes 1983). But Fiat's management too repeatedly and explicitly strove to ensure the credibility of its threat, even appointing a new managing director known for his hard line on labor issues. And while shop stewards and some local union officials never found the company's commitment to redundancies credible, continuing to believe that a last-minute government rescue operation could be engineered (Bonazzi 1984; Carmignani 1984), this does not distinguish the two cases, since management at both firms reported that shop stewards failed to grasp the extent of the danger to the company, endorsing militant strategies despite the more moderate views of both national union officials and the rank and file.

5. *The employee preferences argument:*   Finally, perhaps the reactions of union officials in the two countries differed because employees exhibited different preferences. But here, too, the evidence fails to support the hypothesis.

Even before events unfolded, FLM officials had information indicating that substantial numbers of Fiat employees were likely to view militant opposition to work-force reductions with disfavor. The Italian Communist party had conducted a survey of Fiat employees in the year before the strike. The highly publicized results indicated that the company's manual employees were largely moderate in their orientations to industrial relations, favoring cooperation rather than antagonism between labor and management (Accornero, Carmignani, and Magna 1985, 35). Indeed, if the union hadn't suspected that it would encounter trouble with the rank and file, it wouldn't have turned to the highly atypical tactics used during the strike, tactics that suggested the union knew it lacked majority support from the rank and file. The controversial decision to blockade the factory was revealing of a deeply divided rank and file: why surround a factory with twenty-four-hour picket lines if not to keep some employees from reporting to work? (In fact, toward the end of the strike, groups of workers did try to enter the factory gates.)

All five of the preceding hypotheses can be ruled out because they fail to show variation on the proposed independent variables that corresponds to the variations in observed outcomes for the two cases. At both Fiat and British Leyland, the rank and file appeared relatively moderate and largely unprepared to resist job loss. Moreover, employee views were well known to union officials. In both cases, national union officials appear to have found management's threat fully credible and to have recognized that substantial job loss was inevitable. In both cases, militant and ideological shop stewards nonetheless endorsed active resistance to job loss, even threatening factory occupations.

TABLE 1.   Actors and Their Strategies

		Actor		
		Workers	Shop Stewards	National Union Officials
Case	BL	Acquiescence	Resistance	Acquiescence
	Fiat	Acquiescence	Resistance	Resistance

The strategies adopted by different actors in the two cases are summarized in table 1. The figure highlights the importance of national union officials in determining the different outcomes. The average worker and the modal steward exhibited indistinguishable strategies across the two cases. But in one case, national officials selected resistance to job loss. In the other they chose not to undertake major industrial action.[8]

A Rational Choice Account

The argument I wish to sustain is the following: where a seniority system (or its functional equivalent) exists, the union's reaction to the credible threat of mass work-force reductions will be to permit the reductions to occur; where no seniority system (or its equivalent) exists, the union will attempt to defend jobs, possibly with strike action. Militant resistance to job loss will thus only occur in situations without effective seniority systems.

The reasoning behind the argument is as follows: Microeconomists have developed a number of competing theories to model the preferences of unions (e.g., Atherton 1973; Blair and Crawford 1984; de Menil 1971; McDonald and Solow 1981; for recent reviews, see Hirsch and Addison 1986, chap. 2; Oswald 1986b). One of these—I neglect its rivals entirely here—argues that the union's emphasis on wages versus jobs depends on the presence or absence of a seniority system for layoffs (Oswald 1986a, 1986b). Seniority systems, it is argued, have the following impact on union strategy: "Because even moderately large slumps . . . do not threaten the jobs of the bulk of employees (they know that it will be the young workers whose jobs will be cut), in any trade union with majority voting it is unlikely—so the model argues—that much emphasis will be given to the goal of high unemployment" (Oswald 1986b, 183). In these situations, the union will concentrate on raising wages as much as possible and allow job loss to occur when management decides it is necessary. Thus, "with lay-offs by seniority . . . the union is indifferent about employment" (Oswald 1986a, 79).

We may extend this insight to situations where unions are threatened by mass work-force reductions. Assume that union officials are sensitive to the need to protect shop-floor activists and shop-floor organization. Assume that all levels of the union are committed to maintaining shop-floor organization and that the protection of a network of shop-floor activists constitutes a primary organizational goal, one intimately connected to organizational maintenance (Wilson 1973).[9]

The reasons are readily apparent. "The union participant," one discussion of shop-floor unionism has explained, "is a necessary ingredient without which most local unions could not operate. There must be personnel to fill posts, opinion leaders to inform and stimulate, a cadre to mobilize for the various modes of latent and overt combat" (Spinrad 1960, 244). This is true regardless of the degree of autonomy or importance of stewards in collective bargaining. Even if they lack much power, shop-floor representatives are essential agents of communication with and social control over the rank and file. Activists, moreover, are hard to find; perhaps the single most common characterization of local unions is that they inevitably experience difficulties in stimulating member participation and dealing with the reluctance of ordinary workers to serve as stewards.

Assume next that union activists tend to be drawn from the ranks of more senior employees, by which I mean roughly employees with more seniority than the median. Studies of rank-and-file participation in trade union affairs have generally found that age and seniority are significantly associated with activism (e.g., Anderson 1979; Huszczo 1983; Perline and Lorenz 1970).[10]

Given the relative seniority of union activists and the commitment of national officials to protecting their activists, it follows that national officials will have a greater commitment to protecting the jobs of relatively more senior workers than more junior. In consequence, when a seniority system selects workers for layoff or dismissal—and singles out the most junior and hence least likely to be active in union affairs—the union does not need to defend jobs in order to protect its own factory organization. Where seniority exists, work-force reductions, even when they affect relatively large numbers of employees, will have almost no impact on the union itself. Confronted by a management intransigently committed to personnel reductions, the national union acquiesces, much as occurred, for instance, at British Leyland in the case described above as well as across industries in the United States in the 1970s and 1980s.

However, in situations without effective seniority systems, the union's concern with job loss will be substantial. This will be even more the case when union officials believe that management intends to use personnel reductions to discriminate actively against militants by getting rid of them in disproportionate numbers. Any situation in which the procedures to identify workers to be let go are not already clearly established or in which management refuses to negotiate such procedures in the course of events effectively threatens the organization's activists in this fashion. In this situation, a strike may occur. But it is not aimed at preventing layoffs per se. Rather, *its goal is the establishment or modification of procedures with which to select individuals for dismissal.* Such procedures protect rank-and-file activists from being sacked in disproportionate numbers.

The reason why resistance to job loss elicits such confusion on the part of observers and participants alike is therefore because it is often not aimed at its ostensible, public and articulated goals. In dealing with the rank and file and with the public at large, union officials may claim that they seek to avert layoffs or redundancies. If my argument is correct, however, in negotiating with management, and especially in those meetings not open to public scrutiny, union officials aim instead at establishing procedures for selecting individuals to be laid-off or fired. This discrepancy between the public and the private negotiating goals of the union arises out of the fact that labor may have difficulty making its actual goals public without undercutting its own rank-and-file support; how many workers would stick out a long and desperate strike with the goal of obtaining selection procedures for the dismissal of large numbers of their fellows? To preserve its own negotiating leverage, the union mobilizes the rank and file with the claim that it is seeking to defend jobs. It may do this while also knowing full well that job loss is inevitable.

Assessing the Evidence

If the preceding account is true, union officials cannot express their true goals publicly. A discrepancy exists between the aims of union action and what national officials report. This raises the question of what readers can reasonably expect in the way of evidence corroborating this argument rather than alternative interpretations. It is standard practice in comparative case analysis to investigate directly the intentions of political actors, typically using interviews and direct observation. Should we expect information provided by participants themselves to corroborate the hypothesis advanced here? I believe not.

In principle, if union officials at Fiat aimed to protect shop stewards in the strike of 1980, carefully interviewing these officials could generate evidence to this effect. In practice, however, this procedure is unlikely to prove useful. This is illustrated by the telling reactions of an Italian union official (one intimately involved in events at Fiat) to a version of the argument outlined here (published in Italian in Golden 1989): even if the argument were true, he confessed, he could not corroborate it (interview with Turinese trade union official, February 22, 1980). No responsible union official could publicly confirm that Italy's bitterest strike in three decades could have been avoided if only the union's own shop stewards had been spared at the expense of ordinary workers. And if Italian union officials are unable to verify my hypothesis through direct inquiry, their English counterparts are ill equipped to deny it— for asking union officials what they would have done had a seniority system for layoffs *not* been established at British Leyland is likely to elicit meaningless responses. They do not know, and asking them to speculate about counterfactuals hardly generates conclusive evidence.[11]

Although interview techniques are not likely to be useful, other kinds of evidence can be brought to bear on the problem at hand. If my hypothesis is correct, seniority should have characterized the selection mechanism for layoffs and redundancies at British Leyland but not at Fiat. Next, there should be evidence that union officials in both cases were less concerned with the numbers of employees involved in personnel reductions than with the composition of those to be laid off. In particular, there should be evidence of a special sensitivity to protecting their networks of shop-floor activists, especially shop stewards. Finally, there should be evidence that Italians unions would have settled the dispute had protection for stewards been assured and, conversely, evidence that British unions would have undertaken resistance had it not.[12] I now review what we know against these expectations.

Although it is a legally established criterion used in effecting redundancies (Ventura 1990, sections 6.4, 6.7), seniority does not exist in Italy as a principle regulating temporary layoffs (see Treu 1982). In cases of the latter (i.e., CIG), the selection of employees legally resides exclusively with management. This would suggest the otherwise counterintuitive proposition that Italian unions should oppose temporary layoffs more than redundancies, at least when labor believes that management intends to use layoffs to discriminate against shop stewards.

The public slogan of the 1980 Fiat strike was "No firings!" Privately, however, labor's efforts lay elsewhere. During negotiations prior to the strike, the FLM insisted that layoffs be rotated among workers. The company only threatened redundancies in response to this demand by labor; rotation—indeed, any procedure that infringed on management's unilateral control over the selection of employees to be let go—was considered unacceptable. But as one of the union's leading negotiators explained, "no union, not in Italy, not in Germany or the United States, would have been in a position to make acceptable proposals once the problem was defined this way. It was not simply a matter of reducing personnel (though this was serious and extensive) but of a reduction *that would occur in the ways and on terms decided by Fiat*" (Dealessandri, quoted in Dealessandri and Magnabosco 1987, 93; emphasis added). Corroborating the hypothesis advanced here, the issue that engendered such bitter conflict at Fiat was not job loss per se but rather management's insistence on exercising discretionary selection criteria.

Only after management withdrew the threat to effect redundancies and substituted temporary layoffs did the unions blockade the factory. The ostensibly paradoxical decision to intensify strike action even after the company withdrew its threat to fire was a direct response to management's commitment to unilateral selection criteria and to the repeated refusal to discuss these criteria or even to provide information regarding them. For this and other reasons,[13] organized labor believed the company intended to use work-force reductions to expel shop stewards in disproportionate numbers and to break the union's organization on the factory floor. When the lists of persons laid off were made public, the union maintained that shop stewards, especially the most militant and active among them, were disproportionately affected (Dina 1981, 16–17) and that a preliminary analysis of the data revealed the use of "politically discriminatory and anti-union" criteria (FLM Piemonte n.d., 11). The evidence thus suggests that the union was indifferent to the numbers involved and to whether these were forced redundancies or temporary layoffs. Instead, its principal concern lay with the selection of individuals for layoff, and it was only the use of unilateral selection procedures by the company that caused labor to harden its tactics and blockade the factory.

If the underlying motivation of the strike concerned the protection of stewards, not the prevention of layoffs, did labor succeed? Available data reveal that the company apparently did not use layoffs to rid itself of union representatives in disproportionate numbers. At Mirafiori, for instance, Fiat's largest plant, there was no change in the number of employees represented by each shop steward in the four years before and the three years following the strike (calculated using data reported in Golden 1988, 235, table 29, and 240, table 30). Arguably, the strike helped forestall discrimination along these lines.[14]

However, strike action at Fiat failed in its major goal of securing formal procedures that would permanently protect shop stewards during layoffs. Work-sharing is a common method for reducing production in Italy (see Padoa-Schioppa 1988). Such a procedure protects both workers' incomes and shop stewards, since it strips management of control over the selection of those to be laid off. It was this that the unions so desperately wanted to achieve at Fiat, and this that they failed to obtain.

Ten British Leyland facilities were closed between 1979 and 1986 (company sources);[15] British Leyland's work force fell from 192,000 in 1978—before restructuring began—to 103,000 in 1983 (Willman and Winch 1985, 20, table 2, 2). Only a third of this decline can be attributed to plant shutdowns (Jones 1983, 17; cf. Law 1985, 11); thus, large numbers of employees were let go even in plants still operating. But there were virtually no forced dismissals. With a few exceptions (involving white-collar staff), voluntary redundancies, natural wastage, and early retirements were used instead (company sources; Marsden et al. 1985, 64).

Job loss on such a scale was naturally quite disruptive of union organization on the shop floor. Nonetheless union structures in BL plants survived largely intact. Between 1980 and 1982, for instance, the number of stewards at the company's Longbridge facility fell from 800 to 400 (Willman and Winch 1985, 159). But three-quarters of this is attributable to job loss (see Willman and Winch 1985, 204 n12). The influence of the stewards in shop-floor bargaining and job controls was initially reduced after reorganization, facilities were withdrawn, and the number of senior stewards on full-time release fell substantially (see Seglow and Wallace 1984, 45; Willman and Winch 1985, 159). But interviews with stewards themselves found that "it would be exaggeration to say that the shop-steward organisation at Longbridge was 'broken'" (Willman and Winch 1985, 160, see also 180; also reported in Marsden et al. 1985, 110). By 1982, a new procedural agreement reconstituted steward organization by providing for union checkoff, defining the role of stewards, securing facilities for them, and recognizing the possibility that senior stewards could enjoy full-time release (Willman and Winch 1985, 175). Despite massive job loss, union organization at British Leyland experienced only a temporary curtailment of its influence.

The absence of sustained industrial action at British Leyland despite massive job loss may thus plausibly be ascribed to the relatively weak threat to union organization that such job loss represented. But the best evidence for what unions at British Leyland would have done had seniority procedures not existed comes from looking at what they actually did twenty-five years earlier.

The procedures regulating job loss in the 1970s had been designed in the

1950s explicitly to protect shop stewards (Jefferys 1988; Salmon 1988). In the aftermath of World War II, "questions of managerial control over redundancy and the issue of steward victimization were among the most serious obstacles confronting workplace organisation" (Salmon 1988, 192; also Jefferys 1988, 64). Corroborating the thesis advanced here, research has found that "workplaces did not generally aspire to oppose redundancy as such, but more the method or manner with which redundancy was being carried out" (Salmon 1983, 339). Between 1947 and 1956, there were forty-four strikes against redundancies in the British motor industry. Of these, eighteen were directed against the inclusion of shop stewards on redundancy lists; although these strikes contributed fewer than 17 percent of the total workers involved, they accounted for 58 percent of the working days lost (Salmon 1988, 192). Relatively small numbers of workers undertook relatively lengthy strikes in defense of trade union organization in this period, mainly because management "had a policy of selecting those it wished to be rid of when selecting for redundancy" (company sources, Austin Rover, letter to the author, 1989). And management most wished to be rid of shop stewards, because of the threat that unionization entailed.

Most anti-redundancy strikes failed. But in 1956, a strike at the British Motor Corporation (BMC, later BL) ended with an agreement specifying that seniority would regulate future redundancies (Salmon 1988, 206). The company itself stated that "every reasonable effort was made to observe the principle of 'last-in first-out' . . . [and] approximately 75 per cent of the employees declared redundant had less than three years service with the B.M.C." (BMC 1956, 3).

When it came to management's threats to undertake extensive work-force reductions in the late 1970s, organized labor could justifiably imagine that if redundancies were used, these would occur according to seniority (company sources). Not only had custom and practice long established the use of seniority, but it was guaranteed in numerous written agreements dating back nearly twenty-five years.[16] In sharp contrast to the situation at Fiat, precedent established that work-force reductions take place while protecting union organization on the shop floor. This effectively gave organized labor little incentive to undertake industrial action to resist job loss at British Leyland. In short, union-led industrial action against job loss occurred in pre-seniority British Leyland, and seniority rules at British Leyland were originally established with the intention on the part of the unions of protecting their shop stewards in order to build union organization in the firm.

Concluding Remarks

Evidence corroborates that union-led resistance to work-force reductions are provoked by the fear that such reductions will allow management to pick off shop stewards, thereby breaking the union on the shop floor. One effect of seniority-based layoffs is to prevent industrial action in response to job loss. Indeed, I know of no cases of active and determined union resistance to job loss in Europe, North America, or Japan when manpower reductions have been managed through seniority.

Layoffs in the absence of seniority often occur without triggering industrial action of the kind found at Fiat, however. For active resistance to emerge, union leaders must believe that the firm intends to pick off union activists as it selects those to be expelled from the firm. Historically, firms have been more likely to try to break shop-floor trade unionism in unsettled periods, periods when union recognition and legitimation have been problematic—before unions were accorded full collective bargaining rights, for instance, or when labor's reduced market power inspires especially aggressive managerial behavior. That unions still confront situations that threaten their basic organizational integrity is testament to the fragility of labor's organizational power even in advanced capitalism. Such cases are rare, but deeply revealing of the nature of class relations.

NOTES

1. In this essay, I am not concerned with whether the personnel reductions under consideration involve permanent or temporary termination, an aspect that I argue is not relevant to predicting trade union reactions. For the sake of linguistic precision, I will nonetheless use the terms *redundancy* or *mass dismissal* to refer to a permanent termination of the employment contract, whereas *layoff* will be used to refer to a temporary separation of the employee from the place of work, one that carries with it the possibility of recall.

2. The justification for this assumption is that in capitalist firms, employment levels fall under management's rights and are almost never set through collective bargaining between the parties, as wages almost always are.

3. An alternative view is that of Calmfors and Driffill (1988), who contend that better economic performance is achieved with either a highly centralized or very decentralized bargaining system, but not in intermediate systems. The extent to which variations in union organization or bargaining systems systematically affect economic outcomes remains an unresolved issue.

4. In 1980, Fiat manufactured about two-thirds of Italian-made automobiles; the other Italian producers were small specialist firms, the most well known of which (Alfa Romeo) was subsequently bought out by Fiat. There are no foreign-owned automobile plants in Italy. British Leyland is the United Kingdom's sole major domestic producer. However, much of British-based production is foreign-owned: Ford, Vauxhall (General Motor's British subsidiary), and Talbot all have assembly facilities there. In 1983, BL produced just under half of all automobiles manufactured in the United Kingdom (calculated from Law 1985, 4, table 1).

5. The chronology of events presented in this section has been compiled from Federazione CGIL-CISL-UIL Piemonte 1980; FLM Piemonte n.d.; and Dina 1981. In English, see Hellman 1988, 106–9.

6. The chronology presented in this section is drawn largely from Edwardes 1983; Marsden et al. 1985; Willman and Winch 1985; and the *Financial Times* (London).

7. Interpreting the differences between the AUEW and the TGWU is tricky. The TGWU ostensibly indicated that it was prepared to undertake sustained industrial action in support of the dismissed steward and against work-force reductions, but was prevented from carrying out such a threat by the maneuvering of the AUEW. This assumes that the TGWU was sincerely committed to militant resistance. Equally plausibly, however, the TGWU was able to engage in populist militant position-taking precisely because officials knew that, thanks to the AUEW, they would not be called upon to follow through on their threats. There is no way to discriminate empirically between these two interpretations, since insincere (i.e., strategic) union officials are unlikely to confess publicly. The latter interpretation is required for my argument to hold in full.

8. Despite analytical strictures to the contrary, it is difficult to separate preferences from observed behavior for any of the three actors. (The danger in not doing so is that behavior, rather than reflecting underlying preferences, may reflect sophisticated strategic interaction with another party.) It is especially difficult to do so for national officials.

In the case of workers, survey evidence exists for Italy (Accornero, Carmignani, and Magna 1985) and a series of votes on management's plan for Britain (reported in Willman and Winch 1985, 185, table 9, 1). Both show that the average worker was largely moderate in his orientations to industrial action and likewise that he was prepared to support much of management's plans. Neither source of information is fully independent of observed behavior, but at least both are partially independent of workers' reactions to the threat of job loss.

In the case of shop stewards, interview and survey evidence exists for Italy (Bonazzi 1984; Carmignani 1984) and a series of public pronouncements for Britain (see the sources referred to in note 5). Again, neither is fully independent of observed behavior, and again, the British somewhat less than the Italian. Both show that stewards tended to be substantially more militant than the average worker.

In the case of national officials, finally, there are no sources of information independent of observed behavior in response to the threat of mass job loss. Because union officials know that every word they utter will be scrutinized by management and by rival union officials, there is no way of assessing their sincerity. In the absence of information about the true preferences of national officials, problems of evidence are therefore especially tricky. I consider this more fully below.

9. This does not necessarily imply either that shop-floor activists are democrat-

ically elected or that they are particularly influential in the organization. Rather, it supposes only that national officials recognize the importance of maintaining a functioning organizational network on the factory floor.

10. It seems likely that the relationship between activism and age and/or seniority is parabolic, increasing to a certain point and then gradually dropping off. Among manual employees in the manufacturing industries, for instance, one would expect activism to be most pronounced among mid-career men in their thirties, forties, and even fifties, declining as the anticipation of retirement heightened. I have not seen this hypothesis tested anywhere, but failure to do so may explain why some recent studies claim demographic variables are less important in predicting activism than was previously thought (Anderson 1979; Huszczo 1983).

11. The extremely small number of union officials involved in the relevant events compounds the problem of how to assess the reliability of interview materials for Britain. In Italy, hundreds of people were directly involved in different decisions during the Fiat strike (see Bonazzi 1984; Carmignani 1984), whereas in Britain only a handful were.

12. My argument also requires that shop stewards be relatively senior at Fiat and at BL. Systematic data on steward seniority do not exist. However, analysts of the events at BL have noted a failure of steward organization there to recruit a younger generation in the 1970s (Jefferys 1988, 82), indicating considerable steward seniority. At Fiat the FLM, having recently supervised new elections of stewards, complained repeatedly about the lack of activism and interest in serving as stewards among recently hired employees. (The company had hired some 9,000 new, largely young employees between 1977 and 1979.) All indications are that shop stewards in both cases thus enjoyed relative seniority (i.e., were more senior than the median employee).

13. About a year prior to the strike, Fiat's management had initiated efforts to regain control of the shop floor. This had included dismissing 61 employees. Along with the appointment of a new managing director in the summer of 1980, this convinced many union officials that the company was trying to bust the union on the shop floor.

14. Shop stewards also enjoy some statutory protection in Italy, so laying them off disproportionately could have opened the firm up to legal action. This did not prevent the firm from apparently laying off union members in highly disproportionate numbers, however. In the four largest assembly plants in Turin, for instance, 62 percent of those laid off were union members, out of a work force with a unionization rate of only 34 percent (Bessone et al. 1983, 116, table A, and 117, table B).

15. Interviews by the author with management personnel at the Austin Rover Group (formerly British Leyland) were conducted in 1989, and some of the data reported here was provided then. I am extremely grateful to the company for its help.

16. With the introduction of the Blue Newspaper, management in effect withdrew its recognition of all previously existing written agreements with the unions—but since the unions never accepted the new working and pay conditions described there (where no mention is made of seniority principles), the legal status of "last in/first out" remains ambiguous even today. Court rulings on unfair dismissal claims in the years since then have not resolved whether, in the event of forced redundancies, the company would have to observe seniority (company sources). And, avoiding the legal issues that would inevitably arise were forced redundancies to occur, in the 1980s BL has managed to shed a large part of its work force using other means.

Chapter 3

Why Didn't the Japanese Socialists Moderate Their Policies Much Earlier to Become a Viable Alternative to the Liberal Democratic Party?

Masaru Kohno

Why was the Japan Socialist party (JSP) so slow to moderate its policies, so as to give itself a realistic chance to win an electoral majority and to form a government? According to many observers of post–World War II Japanese politics, it was the failure of this leading opposition party to become a credible alternative to the Liberal Democratic party (LDP) that promoted the fragmentation of the opposition camp and thus prolonged the LDP's single-party rule from 1955 to 1993.[1] Japanese socialists did not discard their Marxist party platform until 1986, and, even then, they clung to their idealistic "unarmed neutralism" with regard to foreign policy. As many aspects of its official doctrine became archaic, the JSP consistently lost electoral support over the years, giving rise to the emergence of small centrist parties and thus diminishing its chances of replacing the conservative government. The JSP did come to power in 1994 when the LDP, which had been ousted from office after the 1993 general election, offered to form a coalition headed by the JSP leader.[2] The alliance with its long-time rival led the JSP finally to abandon its unarmed neutralism, which had served as the ultimate symbol of its postwar progressiveness.

Traditionally, the JSP's long-lasting drift toward the left has been explained in terms of either the legacy of its disastrous coalition experience in the early postwar years, the party's organizational reliance on unionized labor, or its nervousness about (and thus its desire to balance against) the "reactionary" element in the LDP. None of these existing explanations is convincing, however, given the self-defeating consequences of adhering to its leftist policies. This chapter explores an alternative explanation, highlighting the effect of the Japanese electoral system of multimember districts and a single nontransferable vote, which existed between 1947 and 1994. Although some works have already identified the "fragmentation effect" (Reed and Bolland 1991) and the "centrifugal incentives" (Cox 1990) of that electoral system, these general findings have not been used specifically to explain the long-term stagnation of the Japanese socialists. While others, such as Ramseyer and Rosenbluth (1993), point more explicitly to the possible causal link between the electoral system and the JSP's misfortune, no empirical evidence has yet been presented to substantiate their claim. This chapter seeks to offer such evidence. I argue that the JSP's failure to broaden its electoral support originated in the nature of the spatial competition on the left side of the ideological spectrum under the electoral system, that is, the competition between the JSP and the Japan Communist party (JCP). I also demonstrate that the electoral system promoted the fragmentation of the opposition camp and thus further complicated the dilemma of the JSP's electoral strategy.

The argument and evidence presented below have implications beyond the context of postwar Japanese politics. The question of why the Japanese socialists failed for so long to defeat the LDP is important for the study of dominant party systems more generally. While highlighting Japan's distinctive electoral law as the key causal factor, the following exploration is thus an attempt to reveal more general insights about the determinants of such systems.

The next section briefly traces the dominance of the left within the JSP and its consequences on the evolution of the postwar Japanese party system. The third section critically assesses the existing explanations of the JSP's behavior. The fourth section outlines an alternative explanation and provides supporting empirical evidence. The final section concludes with summary and discussion of the broader implications of this chapter.

The Dominance of the Left in the JSP

The Japan Socialist party was created when, in the aftermath of World War II, leaders of prewar, noncommunist proletarian parties agreed to join forces under the expectation that an era of true parliamentary democracy was approaching in Japan. At the earliest stage of the postwar period, the JSP was dominated by moderate "right-wing" elements, such as Tetsu Katayama and Suehiro Nishio, who played a major part in the center-left coalition governments formed in the late 1940s. Katayama, in fact, initially led the coalition as prime minister, until he was replaced by centrist Hitoshi Ashida.

Both the Katayama and Ashida governments, however, were short-lived because the coalition partners had difficulty in reaching policy compromises. Toward the end of Ashida's tenure, a major political scandal surfaced, which involved Ashida himself and several other key cabinet members including Nishio, and thus facilitated the collapse of the coalition. In the following general election held in 1949, the JSP suffered a crushing defeat, reducing the number of its representatives from 144 to 48.

In retrospect, this electoral defeat appears to have had a long-lasting impact on the JSP's policy and organization. At the party congress held after the election, the leader of a leftist faction, Mosaburo Suzuki, was elected for the first time as the party secretary.[3] In October 1949, in the official socialist newspaper, Suzuki elaborated on the rationale for what later became known as "unarmed neutralism," and in December it was adopted as the JSP's official foreign policy (Stockwin 1968). Suzuki's accedence to the party secretary position reflected a more general trend set by the election, namely, the gradual shift of the power balance in favor of the leftist elements within the JSP. The rise of the left intensified the internal rift to the point where the Right-Wing Socialists and the Left-Wing Socialists engaged in separate political activities during the early 1950s.[4] The two Wings decided to reunite in 1955, in response to the prospect of the Liberal-Democratic merger in the conservative camp (to create the LDP). By that time, the relative strength between the left and the right within the JSP had clearly been reversed, in terms of both the vote and seat share (see table 1).

TABLE 1.   The Relative Strength of the Left- and Right-Wing Socialists in the Early Postwar Years

| Year | Left-Wing | | Right-Wing | |
	Seat	Vote Share[a]	Seat	Vote Share
1951	16		29	
1952[b]	56	9.80	60	12.84
1953	72	13.05	66	13.52
1955	89	15.35	67	13.86

Source: Ishikawa 1995.

[a]"Vote share" refers to the percentage of the partisan votes in the total number of votes cast in the election.

[b]The entries for the 1952 seat distribution refer to the numbers of parliamentary members at the time of the party split in October 1951.

The dominance of the left continued for at least the next three decades, surviving a series of internal ideological challenges. In the late 1950s, for example, when the left-right dispute intensified over the revision of the U.S.-Japan Security Treaty, the leftist factions were successful in expelling from the party the rightist faction led by Nishio, who then established the Democratic Socialist party (DSP). During the early 1960s, party secretary Saburo Eda tried to bring about "structural reforms" to the party's platform, but his attempts were ultimately shattered by his rivals at the December 1964 congress. Even more significantly, at this congress, the party adopted a document called "The Road to Socialism" as an official supplement to its platform. This document glorified Soviet socialism and denounced West European styles of social democracies and, as a result, ignited another round of fierce ideological struggles. The document was nevertheless defended intact throughout the 1970s and early 1980s by a group of Marxist-Leninist ideologues called Shakai Shugi Kyokai.[5] Dismayed by the party's inability to change, Eda and his group left the party and created the Social Democratic Front (SDF) in 1977.[6] It was not until 1986 that this archaic document was abandoned under the leadership of Masashi Ishibashi; but, even then, Ishibashi faced insurmountable resistance from the hard-line activists with regard to foreign policy. The JSP finally deserted its unarmed neutralism in 1994, when the Socialist leader Murayama was elected as prime minister to lead the coalition with the LDP.

The JSP's long-term drift toward the left was not electorally beneficial. As documented above, some influential members, like Nishio and Eda, left the JSP precisely because of the JSP's ideological rigidity. Aside from the electoral loss associated with these party splits, the JSP also suffered a long-term decline in its electoral support over the years. In general elections (for the lower house), the JSP's vote share had peaked at 25.3 percent in 1958, after which its electoral support declined consistently (see figure 1).[7] An almost identical long-term decline in the JSP's popularity can be identified in the results of the upper house elections (Ishikawa 1995, 200).

More generally, the JSP's persistent adherence to its original policies had the effect of polarizing the Japanese party system, thus creating opportunities for new parties to enter the electoral competition at the center of the ideological space. The emergence of the Clean Government party (CGP) in the late 1960s and the New Liberal Club (NLC) in the mid-1970s, in addition to the two splinters from the JSP previously mentioned, clearly reflected this niche created by the JSP-LDP confrontation.[8] As the opposition camp became fragmented, the chances of the JSP replacing the LDP in government diminished. Perhaps the only viable strategy left for the JSP would have been to explore a

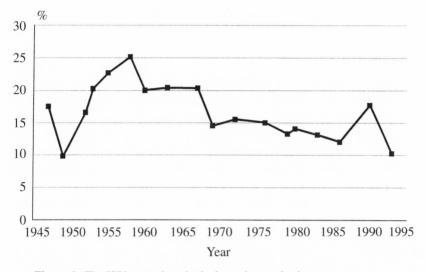

Figure 1. The JSP's vote share in the lower house elections

coalition with these centrist parties, but the JSP's leftist dominance precluded this scenario.[9] Thus, it is not surprising that the JSP was increasingly perceived as a party of perpetual opposition, rather than a party ready to participate in government.

These observations beg two questions: Why did the JSP cling to its leftist policies for such a long period *despite* their apparent negative electoral consequences? And why did the JSP finally abandon the ultimate symbol of its postwar progressiveness, unarmed neutralism, in 1994?

Questioning the Existing Explanations

In the existing literature on contemporary Japanese politics, at least three different explanations can be identified for the JSP's persistent adherence to the leftist policies. Since they are not mutually exclusive, these explanations are often cited simultaneously to complement each other. As argued below, however, none of these explanations is satisfactory.

First, virtually all the studies of postwar Japanese party politics generally and of the JSP in particular point to the JSP's organizational reliance on the militant unionized labor organization Sohyo as the main cause of the JSP's ideological rigidity. This conventional view is well summarized by Flanagan:

One important reason for the Socialists' ideological rigidity can be traced to their organizational dependency on the labor movement. The SP [Socialist party] has often been referred to as a ghost party, with a top-heavy organizational superstructure at the national level but little grass roots organization . . . As a result, the Socialists have depended heavily on their affiliated national union federation, Sohyo, for votes, campaign organizations and workers, funds, and even candidates. (1984, 162)[10]

The second, and much less conventional, explanation for the JSP's persistent leftist tendency highlights the pressure on the JSP to counter the "reactionary" elements within the LDP. According to the main proponent of this view, Otake (1986, 1988), the existence of these elements, together with the fact that the ideological cleavage dividing the LDP and the JSP was so rigid based on issues such as the constitution and postwar settlement, made the JSP overly cautious in dealing with LDP policies and thus prevented the JSP from adopting a more "social-democratic" position like, for example, that of the SPD in Germany. Thus, Otake argues that "the origin of the JSP's tragedy" lay in the nature of Japanese conservatism, rather than in the organizational liability of the JSP itself.

The third explanation for the JSP's failure is more historical and focuses on its disastrous experience of having participated in the coalition governments of the early postwar period. As noted by Stockwin (1986):

[A] steady shift in the balance of power from the Right, which was initially dominant, toward the Left . . . was partly a reaction against the chaotic experience of the Katayama and Ashida governments, in which the JSP had participated under a right-wing leadership. The party was drastically repudiated by the electorate in the aftermath of the Ashida government's collapse, and it recorded by far its worst electoral result up to the present time in the lower house general elections.[11]

What are the problems with these existing explanations? The first two explanations are not convincing, given that the adherence to its leftist policies was hurting the JSP electorally. Both the organizational dependency hypothesis and Otake's conservatism explanation assume implicitly that the JSP was a political party that did not care about elections and voters, an assumption difficult for students of comparative party politics to accept.[12] Furthermore, neither of these two explanations accounts for the JSP's recent abandonment of unarmed neutralism: there is little evidence to suggest that either the JSP's reliance on labor or the influence of the reactionary elements within the LDP suddenly disappeared in 1994.

The only explanation that does take the JSP's sensitivity toward the electorate seriously is the third one; and, as far as the electoral results of the late 1950s are concerned, this explanation is persuasive. There is no doubt that the JSP, as a whole, benefited from leaning toward the left for the four elections after the disastrous 1949 election. But even this explanation falls short because, as shown in figure 1, the benefit of drifting toward the left disappeared after the 1960 election, while the left dominance within the JSP nevertheless continued for many years.[13] We are thus still left with the puzzling question: what accounts for the JSP's adherence to leftist policies, even after such adherence became an electoral liability?

An Alternative Explanation

In their provocative study of contemporary Japanese politics, Ramseyer and Rosenbluth (1993) advance an alternative explanation for the JSP's long-term leftist drift.

> [Another] possibility, and the one we find most compelling, is that a niche strategy of relying on the organizational backing of unionized labor was the logical option for Socialist politicians in Japan's particular electoral system. In a single, nontransferable vote (SNTV), multi-member district system, the equilibrium outcome in spatial terms is for multiple parties to array themselves across the ideological spectrum. (42)

While Ramseyer and Rosenbluth themselves offer no empirical support, this perspective of linking the electoral system and the JSP's behavior is worth exploring for two reasons. First, as described earlier, the JSP's drift toward the left originally began after the general election in 1949, which was the first critical election held under the above electoral system and determined the nature of Japanese party competition for the next few decades to come.[14] Second, the timing of the JSP's abandonment of unarmed neutralism coincided with electoral reform in 1994, in which the system of the SNTV with multimember districts was replaced by a new electoral system.[15] In short, the time span during which the JSP drifted toward the left roughly corresponds to the period during which the above electoral system was in place.[16]

The following analysis begins with an examination of the 1949 election in an attempt to illustrate the nature of spatial competition on the left side of the ideological spectrum that riveted the JSP at the leftist position. I then demonstrate, through both longitudinal and cross-sectional analyses of the JSP's candidate-nomination pattern, how the emergence of small centrist parties during the 1960s further complicated the dilemma of the JSP's electoral strategy.

The 1949 Election and the Communist Threat

In the history of postwar general elections, the JSP suffered its worst defeat in the 1949 election. In the previous election of 1947, the Socialists had received 26 percent of the total vote cast and obtained 143 seats (of the total 466) in the lower house. The JSP had won a plurality, which laid the basis for the two consecutive center-left coalition governments. The 1949 election took place after the collapse of these governments. The JSP's vote share dropped to 13.5 percent, and its seats to 48. The right-wing elements of the JSP were especially hard hit. Both the chairman (and former prime minister), Katayama, and the party secretary, Nishio, lost their seats. Those left-wing members who had participated in the coalition cabinet and were thus considered "pragmatic left," such as Kanju Kato, Masaru Nomizo, and Eiji Tomiyoshi, also lost their seats. Clearly, voters were punishing moderates within the party for making too many policy compromises in the coalition.

Equally noticeable as the JSP's defeat in 1949 was the electoral success of the Japanese Communists. In the previous election, the JCP had only received 3.7 percent of the vote and had obtained 4 seats. In the 1949 election, the JCP received 9.8 percent of the vote and 35 seats. Because the total left vote (including the JSP's, the JCP's, and other small parties') remained relatively unchanged between the two elections, one can speculate that a large portion of votes cast for the JSP in 1947 simply "shifted" to the JCP in 1949. Indeed, according to one estimate, "there is a fairly strong correlation ($r = .51$) between Socialist Party losses and Communist Party gains" (Babb 1992, 29).[17] These observations, together with the fact that the JSP began its drift toward the left immediately after this election, point to a spatial explanation about the JSP's behavior thereafter: it was the JSP's competition vis-à-vis the Communists for the pool of leftist voters that prevented, for many years to come, this leading opposition party from adopting a more moderate social-democratic policy position.

Arguably, if the Japanese electoral system had been a plurality system with single-member districts, the Socialists' move to the left at this point might have been successful in precluding the JCP's threat permanently. That is, assuming strategic behavior on the part of voters, the JSP's move might have led the leftist voters to abandon the Communist candidates who would have had no chance of winning seats under such a system.[18] The actual electoral system in place, however, was one in which voters cast one nontransferable vote to elect several (usually 3 to 5) representatives in each district. Under this system, the "Droop quota" (the proportion of the vote required to guarantee a seat) is significantly lower than that under the Anglo-American plurality system.[19] For the case of the 5-member districts, for example, a candidate was guaranteed a seat with approximately 16.7 percent of the votes in the district. The system thus left opportunities for candidates from small parties, such as the JCP, to compete in the electoral race.

Hence, despite the JSP's attempt to squeeze the JCP out of electoral contention, the latter remained at the left end of the ideological spectrum as a continuing threat for the former. The JCP's threat was formidable especially because the JCP in subsequent years adopted a strategy to nominate candidates in almost all districts, regardless of their individual electoral prospects.

To see how the given electoral system formed the underpinning of the JCP's threat to the JSP, it is important to note that, while the two parties were obvious rivals in many respects, the JSP and the JCP were also engaged in various cooperative efforts during the early postwar years in fostering labor unions and organizing general strikes. Their cooperation was, indeed, not limited to the labor movement, as they were also engineering electoral coalitions, and even merger, in some local districts (Babb 1992, 29). I speculate that, if Japan had adopted a plurality system instead, this electoral cooperation would have been more significant, given that the two parties' electoral strengths and weaknesses complemented each other.[20]

An even bolder counterfactual claim than this can be made, especially in light of two other pieces of evidence. First, in the process of postwar electoral reform (which eventually resulted in the adoption of the SNTV multimember district system), the conservative force repeatedly explored the option of introducing a single-member plurality system, precisely for the purpose of eliminating the JCP from electoral competition. It was only because the American occupation authorities, who were in favor of political pluralism in Japan, vetoed this option that it was not pursued. Hence, it was understood that the fate of the JCP was critically linked with the characteristics of the given electoral system at that time. Second, due to the change in America's overall policy toward Japan, the JCP became the victim of the occupation authorities' "Red purge" in 1950. Subsequently, the JCP had to go through a long dark age during which it adopted a violent political strategy and, as a result, lost much of

**TABLE 2.   The JCP's Seat and Vote Share in the
Early Postwar Years**

Year	Seat	Vote Share (%)
1947	4	2.45
1949	35	7.09
1952	0	1.92
1953	1	1.39
1955	2	1.49
1958	1	1.95
1960	3	2.13
1963	5	2.83
1967	5	3.48
1969	14	4.62

Source: Ishikawa 1995.

its public appeal. As table 2 shows, the JCP's vote share was extremely low
and the JCP could not gain more than a handful of seats in the lower house
throughout the 1960s. If it had not been for the multimember district electoral
system, it is unlikely that the JCP would have survived this crisis and rebuilt
its popular support.

In sum, the election in 1949 was a critical election for the Japanese Socialists. As the JSP suffered such a drastic defeat, the election made clear to
the party leadership the risk of pursuing a liaison with the centrist forces, because the JSP had actually done so from 1947 to 1949. This election, moreover, had a long-term effect because the electoral system in place, that is, the
SNTV, multimember district system, enabled the JCP to maintain its inde-
pendence and to survive the party's crisis of the early postwar years. The JCP's
threat of stealing votes away from the JSP continued and thus riveted the JSP
at the leftist position.[21]

The JSP's Dilemma under the Multiparty System

The electoral system of the SNTV and multimember districts affected the fate
of the JSP, not only because it endorsed the JCP's survival in the early postwar years, but also because it promoted the fragmentation of the opposition
camp, or the emergence of small centrist parties, during the 1960s and 1970s.
As described earlier, two of these parties (the DSP and the SDF) in particular
were the product of defections from the JSP, thus costing the party some
votes-seats associated with the defecting individuals. More generally, how-

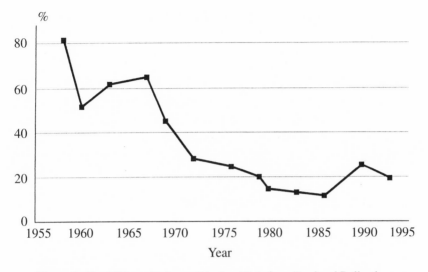

Figure 2. The JSP's multiple candidacies. (Data from Reed and Bolland 1991.)

ever, the revival of the multiparty system had the effect of weakening the JSP electorally, as these new parties presented new policy alternatives within the opposition camp.

I have demonstrated elsewhere (Kohno 1994, 1997) how the existing electoral system affected the process of these centrist parties' strategic entry to the lower-house electoral race.[22] Without being repetitive, let me highlight below how the emergence of these new parties further complicated the dilemma for the JSP's strategy in electoral competition.

It is appropriate to begin the analysis by reviewing the available aggregate data with regard to the change in the JSP's candidate nomination strategy over time. According to Reed and Bolland (1991), in the late 1950s the JSP ran multiple candidates in more than 80 percent of the districts. Because there were only about 130 districts to elect 467 representatives in the lower house, this was a sensible strategy, if the JSP had any intention of winning an election and forming a government. However, the ratio of the districts in which the JSP ran multiple candidates began to decline significantly (see fig. 2).

Why did the ratio of the JSP's multiple candidacy decline? A closer look at figure 2 suggests that the entry of both the DSP and the CGP to the lower-house electoral race had a major impact on the JSP's strategy. There was a considerable drop in the ratio (more than 30 percentage points) from the 1958 to the 1960 election, and this was undoubtedly due to the creation of the DSP. According to the figure, the drop seems to have overshot an otherwise smooth pace of decline, presumably because the DSP was a party created by the defectors from the JSP. The ratio therefore recovered somewhat during the early and mid-1960s, but it again was truncated in 1967, as soon as the CGP entered the lower-house electoral race. As the DSP and the CGP became established, the number of the districts in which the JSP ran more than one candidate continued to decline. Thus, the Japanese electoral system did have a "fragmentation effect," as Reed and Bolland argue, and that effect, in turn, had a negative impact on the fate of the JSP.

The claim that the SNTV, multimember district system facilitated the decline of the JSP's multiple candidacy can also be supported, though more subtly, by the fact that the ratio declined to 12 percent in 1986. On the surface, this number seems *too low,* given that the composition of the Japanese electoral districts was fairly evenly divided between 3-, 4-, and 5-member districts. That is, this low number suggests that the Japanese Socialists faced significant difficulties in fielding multiple candidates even in such large districts as the 4- and 5-member districts. Recall, however, that it was precisely in these larger districts that the newly emerging centrist parties concentrated their candidates in entering into the lower-house electoral race (Kohno 1994, 1997). The multimember structure of the electoral system, therefore, had devastating consequences for the JSP under the emerging multiparty system.

To illustrate the nature of the problem that the JSP was facing, I have investigated the pattern of the JSP's candidate nomination in the 1976 election in some detail. This particular election was selected largely for two methodological reasons. First, in the previous election of 1972, the JCP had made a significant comeback, winning 40 seats. In the 1976 election, therefore, the JCP fielded many incumbent candidates. The existence of these candidates can be used as a reliable measure of the JCP's threat to the JSP. Second, the 1976 election took place when it was relatively easy for observers to identify each JSP candidate with a particular factional affiliation. More specifically, at that time, the right wing consisted of the Eda faction and a group called Atarashii Nagare no Kai, and the left wing consisted of the Shakai Shugi Kyokai group and the Sasaki (Kozo) faction, while the Katsumada (Seichi) faction was placed in the middle.[23]

First, I have compared the districts in which the JSP ran only one candidate with those in which the JSP ran multiple candidates across different-sized districts. The cross-sectional comparison indicates that the size of the districts was a significant factor influencing the JSP's candidate nomination strategy.

Table 3 shows, as expected, that the JSP was less able to field multiple candidates in the smaller districts than in the larger ones.

Second, in an attempt to illustrate the impact of the entry of centrist parties on the Socialist electoral strategy, I have compared the above two categories of districts in terms of the existence or absence of incumbent candidates from the CGP and the DSP (see table 4). The table suggests that the existence of these candidates makes a difference, albeit slight, in the JSP's ability to field multiple candidates. It should also be pointed out that all of the seven districts in which the JSP ran multiple candidates, despite the existence of the centrist incumbents, were 5-member districts. This points to the cumulative effect of the district size factor and the CGP-DSP threat.

The evidence presented so far does not tell one much about why the JSP's policy and organization were dominated by the left elements for so long. A simple answer might be that the DSP was established by splitting off from the right of the JSP and that the JSP's leftist elements were therefore left largely intact. The emergence of the centrist forces, however, must have also meant that the JSP had to face competition from the right, in addition to the already-existing Communist threat from the left, hence further complicating the JSP's dilemma. Given this double bind, what explains the JSP's continuing drift toward the left under the multiparty system?

TABLE 3.   The JSP's Single vs. Multiple Candidacy and District Size

| | Size of the Districts | | | |
	3	4	5	Total
Single	45 (45.9%)	29 (29.6%)	24 (24.5%)	98
Multiple	2 (6.5%)	12 (38.7%)	17 (54.8%)	31
Total	47	41	41	129

Source: Asahi Shimbun, December 4, 1976.
Note: The JSP ran more than two candidates in only one district labeled "Multiple" here.

TABLE 4.   The JSP's Multiple vs. Single Candidacy and Centrist Threat

		Single	Multiple	Total
Incumbent CGP/DSP	Yes	35 (83.3%)	7 (16.7%)	42
competitors?	No	63 (72.4%)	24 (27.6%)	87
Total		98	31	129

Source: Asahi Shimbun, December 4, 1976.

To address this problem fully, one must consider two mutually reinforcing factors. The first is the internal mechanism within the JSP that produced the decline of multiple candidacy. Reed and Bolland call this mechanism "a downward ratchet": "whenever the JSP runs one less candidate than in the previous election, it finds it difficult ever to increase the number of candidates thereafter."[24] But, obviously, the one-way ratchet would not work, if each individual candidate were to ignore the effort at the party level to coordinate the candidate-nomination process and to prevent the disaster of "falling together," or *tomodaore*. Thus, they argue, "the primary mechanism enforcing the downward ratchet in the JSP is the power of incumbents in the nomination process."

By taking this observation a little further, one can argue that the downward ratchet mechanism had asymmetrical consequences for the left and right influences within the JSP. That is, the large number of leftist candidates, who had been elected prior to the rise of the centrist forces in the 1960s, became the beneficiaries of this mechanism internally, as it prevented moderate candidates from challenging them in their individual districts. The notion that the JSP was a party able to coordinate candidate nomination contradicts the conventional wisdom that the JSP was a party of fierce factional and personal strife that hindered party-level decision making. Nevertheless, without assuming some kind of coordination, it is impossible to explain the consistent decline of the JSP's multiple candidacy ratio.

The second factor that explains the continuing dominance of the left is the difference in the electoral strategy adopted by the parties competing with the JSP. To its left, the JSP competed with the JCP, which, as noted earlier, had adopted a strategy of endorsing candidates in virtually all districts regardless of their individual electoral prospects. To its right, the Socialists faced a challenge from the DSP, the CGP, and other small centrist parties, all of which deliberately concentrated their candidates in the larger districts. This asymmetry in the rivals' strategy must have had some impact on the JSP's candidate nomination pattern.[25]

To illustrate this impact, I have used the data from the 1976 election to compare the distribution of Socialist candidates from each ideological grouping in districts that had a credible JCP candidate, on the one hand, with that of districts without a credible JCP candidate, on the other. By "credible," I mean incumbents plus "*jiten*" candidates, or the first runner-up in the previous elections. For the sake of simplicity, I have excluded from the analysis those districts where the JSP ran more than one candidate. According to table 5, however, there is no clear indication that the JSP fielded relatively more left-wing candidates and fewer right-wing candidates in the districts where the Communists posed credible threats.

Because of the centrist parties' strategy of concentrating their candidates in larger districts, I have further investigated the distribution of different types of Socialist candidates across different-sized districts. While the limited number of observations makes it difficult to draw general conclusions, what is striking about this cross-sectional comparison is the total absence of right-wing candidates in the 3-member districts where the JSP had to compete with credible Communist candidates (see table 6).

TABLE 5. Distribution of JSP Candidates from Each Ideological Grouping and Communist Threat

| | | Types of JSP Candidates | | | |
		Left	Center	Right	Total
Credible JCP	Yes	8 (18%)	29 (66%)	7 (16%)	44
candidates?	No	11 (20%)	31 (57%)	12 (22%)	54

Source: Asahi Shimbun, December 4, 1976.

Note: "Right" includes candidates from the Eda faction and Atarashii Nagare no Kai. "Left" includes candidates from Shakai Shugi Kyokai and the Sasaki faction. "Center" includes candidates from the Katsumada faction and those who did not declare their factional affiliation before the election (see also note 23).

TABLE 6. Distribution of JSP Candidates from Each Ideological Grouping, Communist Threat, and District Size

| District Size | Types of JSP Candidates under Communist Threat | | | Total |
	Left	Center	Right	
3	3	14	0	17
4	4	10	2	16
5	1	5	5	11

| District Size | Types of JSP Candidates under No Communist Threat | | | Total |
	Left	Center	Right	
3	6	16	6	28
4	3	8	2	13
5	2	7	4	13

Source: Asahi Shimbun, December 4, 1976.

Thus, under the system of varying-sized districts, the tendency to field leftist candidates (to compete with the Communists) more than canceled the JSP's incentives to run rightist candidates (to meet the centrist challenge), to the extent that there was asymmetry in the rivals' electoral strategy. I conclude that this, together with the power of the incumbents, was at the core of the JSP's dilemma.

Discussion

None of the existing explanations for the Socialists' stagnation in Japan can account for the JSP's puzzling behavior, namely, its long-term adherence to leftist policies despite the negative electoral consequences. In this chapter, I have provided empirical evidence to illustrate the link between the JSP's misfortune and the Japanese electoral system existing from 1947 to 1994. The survival of the Japan Communist party under this system had the effect of riveting the JSP at the left of the ideological spectrum in the early postwar years. The fragmentation of the opposition camp during the 1960s, which was also facilitated by the electoral system, had a complex and even more critical impact on the fate of the JSP: while damaging the JSP's ability to field multiple candidates generally, the rise of the centrist parties, because of the nature of their electoral strategy, still left the JSP an incentive to field leftist candidates. Hence, consistent with the other puzzle-solving chapters of this volume, the Japanese Socialists' behavior as well, which appears to be irrational, is not really so once the full (institutional and other) contexts in which the behavior is embedded are taken into account.

I do not claim that the electoral system was the only determinant of the JSP's behavior. Nor do I consider the JSP's persistent adherence to its original leftist policies *the* rational behavioral outcome that would have necessarily been predicted ex ante based on the formal characteristics of that system. The interpretation presented in the previous section leaves room for some idiosyncratic factors to be relevant. For example, as I have tried to emphasize above, the JSP's original leftist drift was history-laden in the sense that the JSP had to deal with the Communist threat immediately after the disastrous election in 1949. In understanding the JSP's continuing drift toward the left under the revived multiparty system, it was also critical that the JCP, unlike the centrist parties that appeared afterward, adopted the strategy of nominating candidates in virtually all districts. Without understanding the peculiar sequence in which political events actually unfolded in Japan and the peculiar way in which Japanese political actors actually behaved, it would be impossible to reconstruct the ever-changing strategic environment that the JSP was facing and thereby to make sense of its apparently puzzling decisions.

More important, however, the interpretation advanced in this chapter does challenge the notion, often taken for granted in the existing literature on Japanese politics, that the JSP was a party that did not care about voters and elections, or that it was a party too plagued by fierce factional and personal strife to make rational decisions at the party level. Within the confines of the ever-changing strategic environment, the JSP acted in pursuit of its own electoral interests by adhering to leftist policies even though their consequences appear in retrospect to have been self-defeating.

The argument and evidence presented in this chapter can be placed in a broader context. Obviously, the fate of the JSP would have been less tragic if the JSP and other opposition parties could have overcome the obstacles to forming a non-LDP governing coalition much earlier than they actually did in 1993. This points to a more general hypothesis about the determinants of dominant party systems. Simply put, dominant parties, like the LDP in Japan, remain dominant because oppositions fail to coordinate *either* electorally *or* in forging a policy consensus upon which to build a governing coalition.[26] In the Japanese case, it was because the Japanese socialists coordinated their nomination among themselves under the evolving multiparty system that they suffered a long-term electoral stagnation. Some recent studies, in fact, suggest that the degree of nomination coordination within the opposition camp, including the JSP, was more widespread than conventionally believed (Christensen 1996).

Why, then, did the prevalence of electoral coalitions not lead to the formation of a more formal governing coalition within the opposition camp? While it is beyond the scope of the present study, it is worth noting that the ongoing debate about the effect of Japan's electoral system sheds some light on this question. In countering the view held by Christensen and Johnson (1995) that the multimember, single nontransferable vote system had a "super-proportional effect" in producing larger seat bonuses for small parties, Cox (1996) argues that the LDP enjoyed an advantage over the opposition in being able to use pork barrel projects to solve the nomination and vote division problems. The opposition, on the other hand, had to rely on "less effective techniques of dividing the vote, such as allowing their members to carve out ideological niches" (744), thus creating difficulties in formalizing their cooperative relationships.[27] This asymmetry in the available means to overcome the coordination problems must have been at least one important source of the opposition's coalition stagnation.

82   Political Science as Puzzle Solving

NOTES

1. In January 1994, the party changed its name from Shakai-to (Socialist party) to Shakai-Minshu-to (Social Democratic party), although the party's English name had been changed much earlier to the Social Democratic party of Japan. To avoid confusion with the name of another centrist party (Democratic Socialist party, DSP), I will use Japan Socialist party and its acronym JSP throughout this paper.

2. The JSP had participated in the non-LDP coalition government established after the 1993 election. The JSP, however, withdrew from the coalition in April 1994 leaving a fragile minority coalition that fell shortly thereafter. The JSP-LDP liaison developed during this process, and the Socialist leader Tomiichi Murayama was elected as prime minister in June 1994. After nineteen months in office, Murayama was replaced in January 1996 by the LDP leader Ryutaro Hashimoto as prime minister without changing the composition of the governing coalition.

3. Right-wing Katayama remained the party leader, although he lost his seat in the election.

4. Officially, both of these parties called themselves Nihon Shakai-to (Japan Socialist party).

5. Originally a group of intellectuals supporting the JSP, Shakai Shugi Kyokai, the Association of Socialists, had become the voice of the Marxist-Leninist ideologues within the party whose influence expanded significantly during the late 1960s. The ideological and factional conflicts over "The Road . . ." are extremely complex. See Curtis 1988 for details.

6. Eda died, however, immediately after his departure from the JSP without witnessing the official launching of the SDF.

7. In the 1990 election, the JSP's vote share recovered by approximately 6 percentage points (from the previous 12.4 percent to 18 percent) due partly to the popularity of the party's first female leader Takako Doi. This election, however, was an exception. In the following 1993 election, the JSP's share dropped to 15.1 percent and, as plotted in figure 1, this fits well with the JSP's long-term downward trend.

8. The CGP began its political activities as early as the mid-1950s, initially as a political arm of the Soka Gakkai, a lay organization of the Nichiren Soshu sect of the Japanese Buddhism. The NLC was established in 1976 by a handful of politicians who had broken away from the LDP.

9. While Eda made many attempts to explore a left-center coalition during the early 1970s, his growing isolation within the party made these attempts irrelevant.

10. What, then, explains the militancy of Sohyo itself? On this point, some scholars emphasize the fact that Sohyo represented the public sector workers deprived of the right to strike or the right to binding arbitration. Thus, the Sohyo leadership "has continued to view its problems as political rather than economic" (Flanagan 1984, 162). Others focus more historically on the fact that Sohyo was originally organized with the encouragement of the postwar American occupation authorities to compete with the growing Communist influence in the Japanese labor movement at that time (Stockwin 1986). The JCP's bid for control over the newly formed unions was unacceptable to the occupation authorities because of the JCP's claim that the emperor system had to be overthrown.

11. This view, in fact, has been the JSP's own official account of its history. See Gekkan Shakai-to Henshu-bu (1974).

12. Some Japanologists, however, suggest precisely that: "For all of its ideological posturing, the JSP is remarkably cynical about the electorate's interest in party principles. For many JSP politicians, ideological statements primarily serve the purpose of keeping party militants happy. They are gist for party congresses, not for public elections" (Curtis 1988, 146).

13. The apparent drop in the JSP's vote share in 1960 is due to the JSP's split and the creation of the DSP. One must therefore conclude that the JSP benefited by leaning toward the left up until that election.

14. It is true that, chronologically, two general elections preceded this election, one in 1946 and the other in 1947. The 1946 election, however, was held under a different electoral system, consisting of varying-sized multimember districts with each voter casting 1 to 3 votes depending on the size of the particular district. The 1947 election was held under the SNTV, multimember district system, but many Japanese voters at that time had extremely limited information about candidates (and political parties), a majority of whom had never been elected before. In this sense, the 1949 election provided the first real opportunity for the Japanese electorate to hold the incumbent politicians accountable and to exercise their power to punish or reward parties' records and platforms.

15. The new system is a hybrid of the single-member plurality and proportional representation systems.

16. It should be pointed out, however, that, contrary to what Ramseyer and Rosenbluth imply above, there is no formal research that identifies the equilibrium location "in spatial terms" at which each political party positions itself under the Japanese electoral system. Two important previous studies do demonstrate the "fragmentation effect" (Reed and Bolland 1991) and the "centrifugal incentives" (Cox 1990) of that electoral system, but these general findings are not necessarily helpful in revealing the pattern of strategic position-taking of individual political parties along the ideological space.

17. In deriving this estimate, the author notes that "this correlation is based on a simple linear regression of the change in voter support for JSP and JCP vote between the 1947 and 1948 [sic] general elections" (30). Aggregate data as such, of course, constitute only circumstantial evidence for voters' "shift" from one party to another. Babb does offer some district-level data to substantiate the voters' shift, although the presentation of his evidence is not thorough.

18. This is precisely the logic of Palfrey (1984), who challenged Downs (1957) and argued that the existing two parties would not converge at the median voter because of the threat of the third party entry either just to the left of the left party or just to the right of the right party.

19. But, of course, not as low as would have been the case under a proportional representation system.

20. Rural districts, which were the areas of the JCP's weakness, remained the JSP's strengths because of the latter's strong tradition in the farmers' movement.

21. Hence, I do not disagree with the third explanation outlined in the previous section, and I do recognize the long-term "legacy" of the 1949 election in affecting the

JSP's behavior. I emphasize, however, that the source of this legacy was institutional in the sense that it was a product of the given electoral system, rather than psychological in the sense that the JSP "over-learned" a lesson (Sato and Matsuzaki 1986, 17) from the disastrous experience. The latter view leaves room for an interpretation that, in the long run, the JSP leadership was irrational or misguided because of this experience.

22. See also Reed 1991 and Cox 1994 upon which my work is built.

23. The ideological identification of these factions needs some clarification. Relative positions of these factions changed over time, not only because of the earlier departure of the rightist faction led by Nishio in 1960 but also because of the complex process of power struggle in the subsequent years. Thus, for example, Eda had originally been thought to be radical, but in 1976 his faction was regarded as being in the right-wing camp. For similar reasons, it should be noted that, while being characterized as "middle of the road," the Katsumada faction usually formed alliances with the left. Also, the Sasaki faction and the Kyokai group were in the bitter conflict in 1976, although both were regarded as the left-wing factions in the party.

24. They present empirical data which demonstrate that "attempts to reverse the ratchet are seldom successful and often have negative consequences for the party and/or for the individual candidates."

25. This observation, of course, raises a question: why did the JCP, unlike other small parties, choose to run candidates in virtually all districts regardless of their individual prospects? One source of this asymmetry may simply be the difference in the parties' financial resources. That is, the resourceful JCP could afford to run all of these candidates even while knowing that many of them had poor electoral chances. Another explanation may be that the JCP has a different agenda than the other parties in nominating their candidates. For example, it is possible that the JCP, whose financing relies largely on the circulation of its official newspaper, has distinctive incentives to maintain and cultivate membership through vigorous campaigning in each electoral district.

26. This hypothesis is consistent with some earlier studies on other dominant parties. See, for example, Riker's (1976, 1982) account of India's Congress party, Laver and Schofield's (1990, esp. 79–81) discussion on Italy's Christian Democrats, and Crombez's (1996) more general model of minority governments.

27. For more on this topic, see McCubbins and Rosenbluth 1995.

Chapter 4

Why Did the Soviet Empire Collapse So Fast—and Why Was the Collapse a Surprise?

Richard D. Anderson Jr.

When Soviet control of Eastern Europe disintegrated in the autumn of 1989, the sudden collapse surprised not only publics, pundits, presidents, and premiers, but also academic prognosticators. Although Zbigniew Brzezinski (1989) foreordained the fall, by no means did he anticipate an autumn of nations within the few months that separated publication from preterition. In 1989 presidents and premiers were still discussing how to avoid violent Soviet counteraction while easing the two loosest bricks, Poland and Hungary, from the wall cleaving Europe. The possibility that the cornerstone, East Germany, might itself crumble was so remote that in December 1988, German chancellor Helmuth Kohl publicly dismissed talk of German unification as belonging to "the realm of fantasy" (Zelikow and Rice 1995, 62). The realm of fantasy then lay eighteen months ahead.

The policymakers and their academic advisers were often one and the same persons, merely exchanging the open collars of academe for the navy pinstripes of power politics. The collapse took them by surprise because of the human gift for preserving existing beliefs in the face of contrary evidence. As late as 1988 Alvin Z. Rubinstein (1988, 273) won a prize from the profession for a book concluding that "until there is more evidence to the contrary, the assumption here is that he [Gorbachev] is streamlining Soviet strategy to make the USSR an even more formidable competitor." A year later, when Gorbachev had stopped competing, instead withdrawing in barely disguised surrender from one third world conflict after another and tolerating anticommunist upheavals in all the Eastern European allies except Bulgaria (where the downfall was not long in coming), the academics and policymakers changed tack. Trying to reconcile the assumption of Soviet determination to retain the grip on Eastern Europe with the evidence of loss of control, analysts turned to their long-standing suspicion that Gorbachev simply did not know how. Harry Gelman, a CIA pensioner hired by RAND to work on Defense Department contracts, summarized this viewpoint in a passage approvingly quoted in a study prepared for the Undersecretary of Defense for Policy:

> Gorbachev . . . lacked an integrating vision of how to coordinate advance in different spheres simultaneously. In addition, his notion of what he wanted in each arena has been continuously evolving—partly in reaction to the . . . failure of previous efforts, and partly in response to his sense of changing political pressures. (Quoted in Asmus, Brown, and Crane 1991, 1)

Hannes Adomeit, Gelman's younger counterpart formerly employed at the West German equivalent of RAND and now moved to Tufts University, would later uphold this view of Gorbachev. Adomeit endorsed the claim by the former Soviet ambassador to West Germany that "the political leadership in Moscow was no longer guiding the course of events but merely reacting to them" (1994, 201).

This depiction of Gorbachev the bumbling improviser solves neither the puzzle of imperial collapse nor the puzzle of the surprise for policymakers and publics. If Gorbachev was visibly improvising as he went, Kohl should have expected that Gorbachev might indeed move reunification into the realm of reality, as Gorbachev later would. Improvisation, especially of a bumbling kind, should have alerted analysts to the possibility that anything might happen. As an explanation, this portrait of Gorbachev implies merely that he might have tolerated collapse or might have improvised a violent intervention against it; it does not tell us why one happened and the other did not.

Two former National Security Council aides, one now returned to her Stanford professorship in the capacity of provost, one to Harvard, offer another image of Gorbachev that is, however, no more persuasive as a solution to either puzzle. Correctly noting apparently contradictory behaviors by Gorbachev and other Soviet officials and the curious passivity of Soviet policy in Eastern Europe, they attribute these observations to the exceptional complexity of the domestic and international problems facing the Soviet ruler (Zelikow and Rice 1995, 68–86). Of course, the two scholar-policymakers are quite right to argue that by 1989 the Politburo confronted an unusually complicated, demanding policy environment, but a self-contradictory, passive response is no more justified in response to a complex situation than it is to a simple one.

An alternative view of Gorbachev's conduct might start with John Carroll's (1980, 70) comparison of analysis to a magic show. It is not the analyst who works magic by construing the ill-fitting behaviors of the political actor into some conceptually pleasing mosaic. Instead the actor is the magician, deftly manipulating events to some unknown purpose that the analyst, who sits perplexed in the audience charmed by deft sleight of hand, is responsible to infer from the performance. Conclusions that the magician lacks magic simply abdicate the analyst's responsibility. If in place of viewing Gorbachev as determined to retain the Soviet position in Eastern Europe but too unskilled to manage this admittedly difficult task, we instead take to heart Carroll's parable of the magician, then we may usefully ask what Gorbachev did and how what he did could skillfully have advanced some purpose unknown to us but advantageous to him.

To understand Gorbachev's purpose, first we need to reevaluate what purpose control of Eastern Europe served for the Soviet Politburo. It has been assumed that Eastern Europe represented a security glacis, a shield against Western attack, but that assumption imputes to the Politburo the credulity necessary to believe their speechwriters' adversions to impending military attack by an outmanned and outgunned NATO with leaders irresponsible enough to start nuclear war. If that imputation did not stretch credibility enough, the standard assumption faces another paradox: as the increasing Soviet capabilities for intercontinental delivery of nuclear warheads steadily eroded the security value of the glacis, the Politburo proved willing to pay not less but more to preserve it.

To resolve this paradox, one may look not to illusory security benefits but instead to the usefulness of Eastern Europe for domestic political competition within the USSR. The same competitive motives that impelled Gorbachev's predecessors to sustain socialism in Eastern Europe, even at increasing cost in a declining hardship economy, impelled him, with his sharply contrasting domestic strategy, to seek any escape from Eastern Europe even at quite acceptable minor (and it is reasonable to think, even nil) additional risk to the security of his country. The magic of Gorbachev's strategy in Eastern Europe was his understanding that given the previously established institutions for decision making, "action" in his case meant *decisive inaction*. To unload the political yoke with which Soviet control of Eastern Europe burdened him, all Gorbachev had to do was nothing. The loss of control was a surprise because responsible Western scholars and policymakers were unwilling to revise their image of the Soviet Union as a competitor, and the collapse happened because whether the Soviet Union competed in world politics depended on what its leaders were trying to accomplish in domestic politics. When that changed, the world changed.

Economic Subsidy, Domestic Political Competition, and
Soviet Empire

Like the colonial empires of Britain and France, the Soviet empire in Eastern
Europe was unprofitable for the metropole—which is far from saying that any
of these empires were unprofitable for every person in the metropole. The
unprofitability of the Soviet empire raises the question of why the Soviet
Union insisted on keeping it. One argument is that the Soviets were buying
military security. That argument depends on a particular conception of the effects of nuclear weapons; if one thinks, as I do, that adequate stockpiles of nuclear weapons deter attack, then some other argument must be sought. I argue
that the Soviet Union paid for Eastern Europe because the individuals who
decided how the Soviet Union spent its money obtained personal, political
gains in return.

Scholarship has clearly established that at least from the early 1960s on-
ward, the Soviet Union maintained socialism in Eastern Europe by paying an
implicit economic subsidy to five of the six Eastern European participants in
the Council for Economic Mutual Assistance (CEMA), the trading bloc of the
communist countries (Marrese and Vanous 1983; Marer 1984; Marrese and
Vanous 1988). This subsidy inhered in the pattern of trade between the resource-
abundant Soviet Union and the resource-poor Eastern European partners, especially East Germany, Poland, Czechoslovakia, and Hungary. The Soviet
Union delivered fuels and raw materials in return for Eastern European manufactures, with the exchange prices determined by valuing both sides' goods at
CEMA foreign trade prices. CEMA set prices for fuel and raw materials below
world market prices, while setting prices for manufactures above world market prices. Consequently the Soviet Union was subsidizing the Eastern European countries by the amount of the difference between CEMA prices and
world market prices. With commodities depreciating relative to manufactures
in world trade, the combination of more rapid inflation of CEMA prices for
manufactures with more rapid depreciation of CEMA prices for commodities
caused this subsidy to increase steadily. Disagreement continues about the
scale of the subsidy, especially because the international commodity market is
hardly perfect and the unloading of Soviet exports to Eastern Europe onto the
world market would have depressed prices, but no one questions either the fact
of the subsidy or its steady growth.

The economic liability of possession of Eastern Europe raises the question
of identifying noneconomic benefits received in return. Normally observers
suggest that a variety of benefits accrued to the collective Soviet agent. Secu-

rity typically ranks high in lists of these benefits. Possession of Eastern Europe is said to have augmented strategic depth for the Soviet Union, diminished it for the European capitalist states, and provided an example for the Soviet Union's global alliance (Brown 1988, 30–32). By controlling Eastern Europe the Soviet Union kept NATO's largest concentration of ground and air forces at a distance from its own frontier. Deployment of Soviet units, equipped with the most modern weapons in the Soviet arsenal and kept at the highest peacetime readiness of any Soviet forces, also brought the English Channel within reach of a rapid advance. Not only would the reduction of NATO's strategic depth secure a decisive advantage in war, but the threat of the dash to the Channel earned a controlling say over the diplomatic agenda in Europe. The Eastern European states' alliance with the USSR offered a model for emulation by states in the Third World (such as, at different times, Egypt, Iraq, Afghanistan, or Angola) where radical leaders aspired to Soviet-style socialism.

Whether one accepts that the subsidy purchased security for the Soviet Politburo depends on one's view of the consequences of the deployment of nuclear weapons delivered by ballistic and cruise missiles with intercontinental range. By one argument, when both superpowers deployed these missiles in growing numbers, their respective deployments were mutually nullifying. Nuclear weapons in the possession of one side deterred the use of nuclear weapons by the other side. The nuclear standoff made possible, and perhaps positively encouraged, warfare with conventional weapons. By this argument, as U.S. and Soviet nuclear stockpiles expanded between 1960 and 1985, strategic depth and global alliances retained their previous usefulness for enhancing security.

The other argument holds that deterrence by nuclear weapons extended to conventional warfare, too, certainly not all the way down to deterring conventional invasions of territory not a vital interest of the other superpower (e.g., Afghanistan for the United States, or Grenada for the Soviet Union), but down at least as far as vital territories defended by conventional military tripwires. By this argument, strategic depth and global alliances steadily lost value as the capability of either side to launch retaliatory strikes increased. Strategic depth and global alliances provided the Soviets no defensive advantage, because neither could prevent penetration by missiles carrying warheads capable of devastating the homeland, while neither NATO's lack of depth nor Soviet base rights around the world provided any offensive advantage, because Soviet exploitation of it risked the same devastation.

The observation that the Brezhnev Politburo authorized deployment of additional nuclear weapons between 1960 and 1980 while steadily increasing the scale of the implicit subsidy to Eastern Europe might be taken as evidence favoring the argument about nuclear deadlock. Why pay more for strategic depth if it is losing value? But if the extended deterrence argument is correct, the Brezhnev Politburo was buying something other than strategic depth in Eastern Europe.

Without pretending to resolve the argument over deterrence, I would suggest that communist rule in Eastern Europe also offered individuals in the Brezhnev Politburo, and more broadly in the ruling bureaucracy, political advantages that made it worthwhile for them to approve subsidies to Eastern Europe, especially since these subsidies could be hidden from most Soviet officials by pricing arrangements that made the subsidies look like equal exchange.

The individual benefits to Soviet leaders provided by communist rule in Eastern Europe became visible when Brezhnev assumed the leadership of the Soviet Union in 1964. Over the next year, together with a few allies he challenged economic reforms advocated by the majority of the post-Khrushchev Politburo, and in particular by his leading rival Aleksei Kosygin. All parties to this contest advanced public justifications of their preferred policies. Like U.S. politicians who make the case for industrial policy by citing the economic success of Japan, or for welfare programs by citing the social peace of Sweden, the Politburo members drew attention to the experience of foreign countries. Their discussion of this experience served to bolster the arguments for their own preferences and to undermine the persuasiveness of their opponents' case.

By the conventions of Soviet politics at the time, capitalist practices were normally to be cited in domestic debates only as negative examples to be avoided, not emulated. Thus Brezhnev's bureaucratic supporters warned that the economic reforms advocated by Kosygin threatened subversion of a socialist planned economy by allowing the penetration of illegitimate capitalist practices like profit-making, marketing, and interest charges. Kosygin and his backers defended themselves by pointing to the Eastern European communist allies. In all five of the loyal countries, economic reforms comparable to those advocated by Kosygin were being introduced or extended during 1965. By pointing to the Eastern European examples, Kosygin was able to counter accusations that profits, markets, and interest were unsocialist by calling attention to these practices in the unquestionably socialist Eastern European states.

Meanwhile a similar argument was proceeding over Brezhnev's proposals for increased investment in agriculture, a sector considered by Kosygin unlikely to produce rewards sufficient to justify the expenditure. Brezhnev defended his proposals in part by pointing to the effectiveness of increased investment in Bulgarian agriculture.

If the subsidy to Eastern Europe purchased the maintenance of socialism there, with the benefit to all sides in Politburo arguments of making socialist cases available for use as positive models in bolstering claims for their preferred policies, then Brezhnev's contest with Kosygin should have shaped their attitudes toward the subsidy. During 1965, when Eastern European reforms were legitimating Kosygin's political strategy, Brezhnev publicly advocated cutting the implicit subsidy to Eastern Europe. He called for an increase in the share of manufactures in Soviet exports to the Eastern Europeans. As trade with Eastern Europe was then constrained by a rule of bilateral clearing, to balance the increase in Soviet deliveries of manufactures the Eastern Europeans would have needed either to deliver more manufactures in return or to accept smaller quantities of fuels and raw materials. Either way the subsidy would have declined relative to total trade, and predictably the leaders of the three countries that were the main beneficiaries—Gomulka of Poland, Novotny of Czechoslovakia, and Ulbricht of the German Democratic Republic (GDR)—publicly protested Brezhnev's demands. Their position obtained an endorsement from Kosygin, who appealed publicly for an increase in "specialization and cooperation" among socialist countries. Since the abundant resource endowment of the Soviet Union was understood to require it to specialize in supplying fuels and raw materials, his proposal signified an increase in the implicit subsidy.

The outcome of the dispute was a draw. Speeches in 1965 concerned the plan for exchanges in 1966. Measured in rubles, Soviet fuel and raw material deliveries remained constant while exports of manufactures increased substantially in 1966 over 1965. While this outcome favored Brezhnev, offsetting cuts in Eastern European exports to the Soviet Union combined with changes in the world market value of Soviet exports to increase the subsidy measured in dollars. That outcome favored Kosygin and the Eastern Europeans, although to most audiences for Politburo politics inside the Soviet Union, of course, the dollar valuation was invisible while the ruble valuation was prominent (Anderson 1993, 108–10).

The hypothesis that communist regimes in Eastern Europe produced individual benefits to Politburo members explains not only the configuration and outcomes of the Kosygin-Brezhnev dispute over the subsidy in 1965 but also the sharp expansion of the subsidy after 1973. From the perspective of accounting, the increase of the subsidy measured in dollars was due to the 1973 doubling of the world price of oil, which composed a significant proportion of Soviet deliveries. At the same time, a political decision by the Politburo was required not to take more complete advantage of the opportunity to shift oil exports from Eastern Europe to the world market, where oil sales could have earned significantly more. Having won his contest with Kosygin by 1971, Brezhnev was now in a position to force that decision.

But changes in Eastern Europe had altered Brezhnev's attitude toward the subsidy. Military intervention in Czechoslovakia in 1968 had replaced the economic reformers there with counterreformers who took power in 1969 and worked diligently to reverse reforms over the next three years. Brezhnev's refusal to support Gomulka against rioting workers in December 1970 forced him to cede to Eduard Gierek, who abandoned reforms in favor of embarking on the international borrowing made possible by Brezhnev's new policy of East-West détente. Ulbricht's resistance to the German component of Brezhnev's East-West reconciliation exposed him to a challenge from his erstwhile deputy Erich Honecker in May 1971, and Honecker, previously an advocate of economic reforms, now reversed them too. In Hungary in 1972 Soviet pressure forced Janos Kadar to abrogate the reform program as well, although he managed to retain office; Bulgaria had already given them up on its own. With all the Eastern European leaderships now solidly in the antireform camp, the subsidy would buy favorable evidence for Brezhnev's preferred policies, and this gain to him was worth forgoing additional earnings for the Soviet Union in the world energy market. Since Eastern European policies were now bolstering Brezhnev's political strategy, Kosygin began trying to limit the subsidy by demanding a revision of pricing procedures in CEMA, but Brezhnev's predominance in the Politburo enabled him to maintain a subsidy more than five times its dollar value in the 1960s.

Not only Politburo members found possession of Eastern Europe useful in bureaucratic politics. The military was claiming a steadily rising share of the national income to purchase both nuclear weapons and equipment for ground and naval forces. The high command justified its procurements by promulgating an offensive, war-winning strategy that took advantage of the widely held belief that offensive action in war requires more force than defense. By reducing NATO's strategic depth, deployment of air and ground units structured for offensive action in East Germany lent color (not reality) to military claims that such a strategy could bring victory in a European war. Other bureaucratic interests also exploited the policy of regular contacts between Soviet offices and their Eastern European counterparts, known as "exchanges of useful experience," to encourage the Eastern Europeans to follow policies, the effectiveness of which the Soviet officials could later claim to have been proven under socialist conditions.

Of course, Eastern European examples that lent persuasiveness to the advocacy of one set of Soviet bureaucrats did corresponding harm to the claims of those bureaucrats' domestic rivals, but a compromise could always be reached by a side-payment to the losing bureaucrats. The cost of this side-payment could be imposed on the hapless Soviet consumer, whose interests were represented at best indirectly in the bureaucratic debates. Like English and French colonialism, paid for by taxing those countries' consumers to the benefit of some members of mercantile and official classes, Soviet control of Eastern Europe both reallocated income within the bureaucracy and transferred income to it from the consumer.

Gorbachev and the Collapse of Eastern European Communism

The economic recession confronting Gorbachev when he took power in March 1985 provides a plausible inducement for him to seek policies that would let him reduce military spending and end costly subsidies to an array of foreign allies, not only in Eastern Europe but also in Central Asia, Africa, Southeast Asia, and the Caribbean. Gorbachev's effort to negotiate a global settlement with Presidents Reagan and Bush, as well as his fire-sale approach to German reunification, can be interpreted as products of an effort to manage the economic situation, especially as the crisis steadily worsened under his stewardship. But if the economic crisis motivated Gorbachev's decisions, it is hard to understand why he chose policies that exacerbated it. Of course, if we view Gorbachev as a skilled tactician without strategic vision, then a combination of intent to improve the economy with policies that made it worse makes eminent sense. But as Baruch Fischhoff (1982, 340) remarks, "Upon careful examination, many apparent errors prove to represent deft resolution of the wrong problem." The problem Gorbachev deftly resolved was not even the "wrong" one. The right problem was emancipation of the Soviet people from the Soviet order, and the economic crisis of the old order was not a problem for Gorbachev but an opportunity. It gave him the lever with which he pried loose the dead hand of Soviet bureaucrats.

Gorbachev chose political change over economic improvement. Saying that he was trying to induce recalcitrant bureaucrats to change behaviors profitable to them but corrosive to performance of the economy as a whole (including but not confined to the subsidy to Eastern Europe), Gorbachev for the first time encouraged spontaneous political activity by the general Soviet population. He spoke of containing this activity, of channeling it within the bounds of his program of perestroika, but whenever popular political activism exceeded the limits he had previously set, Gorbachev responded by extending the limits to encompass the latest popular initiative. This habit earned his strategy the label "radical centrism" or "dynamic centrism" in the work of various Western observers not caught up in insisting that Gorbachev was just an improviser, and by 1990 even Gorbachev was calling himself a "centrist" (Breslauer 1989; Roeder 1993).

In what sense was his strategy centrist? Gorbachev sought to pose a choice both to Soviet bureaucrats and to the Soviet citizenry. The bureaucrats' choice was to comply with Gorbachev's program or face the manifest antagonism of a citizenry that had abandoned the sullen passivity, intermittently interrupted by wildcat strikes or localized riots, characteristic of its behavior since Stalin's repression had demonstrated the futility of open opposition. The citizenry's choice was to tolerate Gorbachev's leadership or face a renewal of repression by bureaucrats terrified of popular hostility.

The literature raises various possible goals that Gorbachev may have been trying to reach by this strategy. Hough (1989) insists that he sought no more than for the threat of popular retaliation to compel bureaucrats to refrain from sabotaging his managerial reforms intended to restore the international competitiveness of the laboring Soviet economy. Perhaps Gorbachev was a constitutional reformer using popular mobilization to emancipate himself from the restraints imposed by collective leadership in the Politburo and dependence on the selectorate called the Central Committee (Roeder 1993). Conceivably, even, Gorbachev wanted to introduce democracy for its own sake, in the recognition that, as Richard Lowenthal presciently argued two decades ago, no polity can legitimate itself forever by performance and its leaders must therefore ultimately seek popular consent to their rule (Lowenthal 1974; Gooding 1990).

Like Brezhnev, Gorbachev faced both opponents and allies in the Politburo. The opponents were led by Egor Ligachev and Nikolai Ryzhkov, who shared Gorbachev's goal of reviving the economy by means of a Kosygin-style reform but who differed with him over the merits of mobilizing popular discontent. Ligachev, in particular, preferred the imposition of stricter discipline on the populace, for example by means of the antialcoholism campaign that he inaugurated in 1985. His and Ryzhkov's calls for imposition of discipline were endorsed by a majority of Politburo members as late as 1989, even though Gorbachev was saying that order could be restored only by relying on popular activism.

Developments in Eastern Europe could either help or hinder Gorbachev in his contest with the Politburo conservatives. To win the contest, Gorbachev needed to alter the calculus, by both citizens and bureaucrats, that had produced the combination of popular passivity and bureaucratic obstruction characteristic of the Soviet Union at the end of the Brezhnev years. In general, calculus of cost and benefit is inadequate to generate collective political participation on the scale that Gorbachev tried to inspire. The individual citizen faces a choice between joining demonstrations and staying home or between voting and staying home. If enough others demonstrate or vote, the citizen will receive the benefits of demonstrating or voting and can avoid any cost, while if not enough others demonstrate or vote, the individual citizen cannot accomplish the purpose regarded as beneficial and may as well avoid the costs. Understanding, at least implicitly, this "paradox of collective action," Gorbachev sought not to reward participation but to inspire it, first by his personal charisma and then, as that faded, by tolerating the charismatic leadership of democrats, including Boris Yeltsin, even when they built it by voicing popular dissatisfaction with Gorbachev himself. While collective action must depend on inspiration rather than calculus of cost and benefit, however, the *scale* of collective action is not independent of its costs and benefits. At the margin fewer people will participate where action is more costly or less beneficial (Grofman 1993a).

Gorbachev could obtain more collective action in the Soviet Union if he manipulated costs and benefits for both Soviet citizens and Soviet bureaucrats. Citizens can be assumed to have been less willing to demonstrate if they expected to encounter police repression and more willing to demonstrate if they expected to achieve dramatic political change. Bureaucrats can be assumed to have been more willing to engage in violent repression if they expected a triumphant citizenry to take violent revenge on them and less willing to repress if they expected political change to advance their careers—either by making space for promotions by removing their superiors from office, or by offering opportunities to raise their incomes by allowing them to become private entrepreneurs. Actions in Eastern Europe could convince both Soviet audiences, habituated by experience to perceiving Eastern European developments as information about the Politburo's course in domestic policy, that either repression or dramatic political change was impending. If Soviet citizens saw military intervention against demonstrators in Eastern Europe, they could expect the costs of demonstrating to be high and the demonstrations to be ineffective in accomplishing political change. If repression did not occur and communist rulers in Eastern Europe lost office after the demonstration, the converse inference would be warranted.

Soviet political institutions offered Gorbachev the opportunity to change estimates of costs and benefits by potential demonstrators at home and abroad.

Gorbachev exercised this capacity despite the Party Rules, by which a simple majority of Politburo members (who numbered twelve in 1989) sufficed to adopt any decision and by which he cast only one vote. (In practice, as confirmed by reports from the Khrushchev, Brezhnev, and Gorbachev eras, whenever there was significant dissent decisions were referred to subcommittees of the Politburo for compromise resolutions before being returned to the Politburo agenda for action.) Majority rule in the Politburo was counterbalanced by the General Secretary's predominant influence over the agenda. By the Party Rules any member of the Politburo enjoyed the right to raise issues for consideration, but by secret instructions the General Secretary decided who received what kinds of information from the Central Committee staff departments under his supervision. Consequently, if a Politburo member raised an issue other than those about which the General Secretary had authorized the member to receive official information, the General Secretary could credibly reply that the member was uninformed about the issue. By this device he could prevent its consideration. In effect, the procedures gave the General Secretary virtual veto power over the Politburo agenda. Gorbachev's opponent Ligachev occupied the powerful post of "second secretary," responsible for all personnel appointments, but even in this post, he writes, Ligachev restrained himself to the exercise of the right of any party member to send a letter to the General Secretary requesting Politburo consideration of an issue. Gorbachev simply never forwarded Ligachev's letters to the rest of the Politburo membership (Ligachev 1993, 113–18).

In addition to veto power over the Politburo agenda, the General Secretary also exercised special responsibility for Eastern Europe. On the desks of the heads of the communist parties in Berlin, Budapest, Prague, Sofia, and Warsaw sat secure telephones connecting directly to the desk of the Soviet General Secretary in the Kremlin. No significant policy decision or official appointment could be decided without prior clearance by the General Secretary (Mlynar 1980). Control over appointments enabled successive Soviet leaders to subject Eastern European party chiefs to discipline. By forbidding the Eastern European party chiefs to remove their domestic enemies from power, the Soviet General Secretaries ensured that a mere signal of withdrawal of support from the local party chief would produce a revolt against him within the leadership of the local party.

The General Secretary's effective veto power over the Politburo agenda and special responsibility for liaison with Eastern Europe's capitals enabled Gorbachev to encourage demonstrators in Eastern Europe and to discourage bureaucratic repression. All he had to do was nothing.

Why could Gorbachev's inaction have been so decisive? If demonstrations began in one of the five Eastern European countries subject to Soviet controls, the head of the local Politburo could not take repressive action without permission from Gorbachev. If asked for permission, Gorbachev could simply answer that he needed to consult the Soviet Politburo—and then fail to consult. Receiving no answer from Moscow, members of the local Politburo would discern that the local chief had lost the confidence of the Soviet General Secretary. Because of the risk that no answer would be forthcoming from a request, the head of the local Politburo might choose to refrain from asking permission to repress riots. Then the absence of repression would signal to the crowds that the costs of demonstrating were low, encouraging people to swell the crowds. As demonstrations spread, frightened members of the local Politburo would demand the resignation of the local party chief, who as the most visible member of the local leadership bore the brunt of popular dissatisfaction. Either way, given Gorbachev's decisive inaction, demonstrations in Eastern Europe would not suffer repression and would accomplish visible political results—the removal of a national party chief. The absence of repression would combine with the achievement of results to send an encouraging signal to potential demonstrators in the Soviet Union.

Statements by Gorbachev's allies in the Politburo, commentary by his opponents in the Politburo, and his own utterances during meetings with the East German leaders manifest the interaction between inaction in Eastern Europe and popular mobilization in the Soviet Union. One of his principal allies was Eduard Shevardnadze, who would later write (1991, 14): "If you begin democratization of your own country, you don't have the right to block this process in other countries. And if you reject adherence to the 'philosophy of tanks' in relation to neighboring countries, then as a minimum you must not think in its categories in relation to your own country."

Gorbachev's opponents were equally well aware of the connection between Eastern European events and domestic mobilization. Ligachev and Ryzhkov were trying to disrupt Gorbachev's domestic strategy by attempting to persuade Soviet consumers that existing political institutions could improve their standard of living in return for continuing political passivity. Ryzhkov's method was to promise a reorientation of industry toward consumer goods, while Ligachev's was to claim that collective farms under proper management could achieve an improvement in the Soviet diet. To bolster this argument (which must have been remarkably unpersuasive), as late as September 1989 Ligachev reverted to the Brezhnev-era technique of citing Eastern European experience:

Our delegation has studied the GDR—and incidentally, studied somewhat earlier in the CSSR—questions connected with the realization of agrarian policy, questions connected with the social rearrangement of the country-side. I must note with great satisfaction that we have seen time and time again, both in the GDR and in Czechoslovakia, that it is possible to resolve, on the roads of socialist development, fundamental questions related to social and economic rearrangement of the countryside and to supply one's peoples fully both with a good quality and with a broad range of food-stuffs. (Moscow Television Service, September 15, 1989, in FBIS-SOV, September 18, 1989)

This statement not only bolstered Ligachev's promise of an improved diet. The reversion to the rhetoric of the Brezhnev era also signaled that nothing was changing in Eastern Europe. But within ninety days the possibility of follow-ing "roads of socialist development" had been decisively rejected in both East Germany and Czechoslovakia.

An analysis of the interaction between Gorbachev's domestic strategy and the collapse of Eastern European communism raises a question about what out-come he wanted there. A reasonable assumption is that he sought the replace-ment of the orthodox communist regimes installed by Brezhnev with regimes led by reform communists of his own stamp. In support of this assumption, one may note that Honecker had lent aid and comfort to Soviet conservatives, openly warning against Gorbachev's reforms and conspicuously banning the circulation of Soviet publications in East Germany. But the validity of this as-sumption depends on what Soviet citizens wanted. If the prospect of reform communism was sufficient to motivate them to take to the streets in opposition to Gorbachev's conservative rivals, then the sight of reform communists taking power in Eastern Europe would have accomplished Gorbachev's ends. But if Soviet citizens wanted to expel communists from power entirely, then for the attainment of a popular movement at home sufficient to counterbalance against the bureaucratic opposition led by Ligachev and Ryzhkov, Gorbachev would have wanted to raise the Soviet people's hopes with the sight of a communist collapse. At the same time he needed to keep Soviet bureaucrats from observ-ing their Eastern European counterparts suffering the public reprisals which they themselves feared. The determination of the East German demonstrators to refrain from violence against the state heightened the persuasiveness of Gor-bachev's appeals to bureaucrats to surrender power.

The record, such as it is, of Gorbachev's conduct toward Eastern Europe is consistent with the argument that he favored the collapse of communism there and sought to achieve it by refraining from violence. The only record consists of utterances, whether private or public, addressed by Gorbachev or his spokesmen to various audiences: Eastern European publics, Eastern European leaders, Western leaders, Soviet publics and leaders. As the basis for Adomeit's charge that Gorbachev was merely improvising, he assumes that such utterances represent Gorbachev's actual thinking—that when Gorbachev spoke to Honecker, his successor Egon Krenz, or the West German Foreign Minister Hans-Dieter Genscher, he disclosed his real thoughts. But if Gorbachev was a centrist, trying to move both bureaucracy and citizenry toward goals he wanted by using the threat of each to influence the other, he should have framed his utterances for the sympathy of both sides. Since Gorbachev knew the sides' purposes were incompatible, frankness should have been furthest from his mind. And therefore Gorbachev spoke to reduce the cost of participating for citizenry while minimizing the amount at stake for the ruling bureaucracy.

Trying to reduce the costs of demonstrations to East German citizens, Gorbachev met with Honecker and the East German leadership on October 7, 1989, two days before the decisive mass march in Leipzig. When the East Germans tried to turn the discussion toward Soviet help in suppressing the rising swell of demonstrations and marches, Gorbachev avoided answering. Instead he simply changed the topic, seeking the Germans' sympathy by describing how he too faced popular unrest in Moscow. Trying to prevent Soviet bureaucrats from promising to help repress the demonstrators, he then told his embassy staff: "Give no advice! Listen, but don't comment!" When Krenz approached the Soviet ambassador for advice, the ambassador ignored Gorbachev's words while complying with his intent. He told Krenz: "Under no conditions resort to repressive measures, certainly not by the army." Moreover, the ambassador ordered the Soviet commanding general to confine his troops to the barracks (Maier 1997, 156). Demonstrators in Leipzig, one of them told me later, noticed that the ordinary Soviet military traffic was conspicuously absent from their roads. They took heart.

Having encouraged the demonstrators by doing nothing, Gorbachev also reassured bureaucrats in the Soviet Union and East Germany with avowals that nothing would happen. Krenz sought to use the crisis to oust Honecker, but success would serve him only if he could preserve an independent East Germany. The greatest danger to Krenz and other East German bureaucrats was reunification. Less than a week before demonstrators tore down the Berlin Wall, Gorbachev soothed him: "There is no reason to surmise how the German question will be solved some time. The current realities have to be taken into account. This is the important thing." As for the present, Gorbachev said, various Western leaders "proceed from the [desirability of] safeguarding the post-war realities, including the existence of two German states. Posing the question of the unity of Germany is being regarded by all of them as extremely explosive for the current situation" (quoted in Adomeit 1994, 215–16). If, hearing these reassurances, Krenz and Honecker's other rivals saw opportunities to preserve themselves without repressive violence, then Gorbachev's utterances lessened East German bureaucrats' motive to repress. He staged the same performance for Soviet conservatives, exploding in an appearance of fury at Genscher on December 5, 1989, when the West German came to discuss Kohl's proposals for "confederation" with the GDR (Cherniaev 1993, 307–9).

The communist collapse in Eastern Europe helped to sustain reform communism in the USSR by proving that popular action could accomplish dramatic change and by relieving bureaucrats' fears about their prospects in a postcommunist state. When in August 1991 some leading Soviet bureaucrats decided that they could not tolerate a continuation of Gorbachev's leadership, his inaction in Eastern Europe paid off. When they staged a coup, Moscow demonstrators instantly took to the streets in a behavior that Gorbachev had encouraged by his decisive inaction in Eastern Europe. Even though Gorbachev himself had to surrender power, the coup, which he had feared from the beginning and which was the only means of stopping his democratization, failed.

Conclusion

My perspective on the collapse of Eastern European communism instantiates George Tsebelis's (1990a) concept of a nested game. Gorbachev's decisive inaction overturned Eastern European communism not because he cared about social development in Eastern Europe but because his actions, or in this case inaction, toward Eastern European communists promised to affect a game vitally more important to him: the interaction between the bureaucracy and citizenry in the Soviet Union. The same nested game had induced both Khrushchev and Brezhnev, following domestic strategies the opposite of Gorbachev's, to sustain communist rule in Eastern Europe by controlling appointments, by providing subsidies, and by ordering military intervention. By decisive inaction that enabled popular demonstrations and elections to achieve the removal of communists from power in Eastern Europe, Gorbachev encouraged his own citizens to believe that they could attain similar goals in the Soviet Union. The citizens' growing belief in themselves, sustained by the sight of popular action in Eastern Europe, helps to explain both why hundreds of thousands of them stood outdoors in the cold of February 1990 to pressure the Central Committee into accepting Gorbachev's proposal for multiparty politics and why another hundred thousand would rally to the Russian White House in August 1991 behind a demand to protect Gorbachev as the constitutional president against an unconstitutional emergency committee.

The collapse of Soviet empire in Eastern Europe happened fast because the organization of power in the Soviet Union put the decisions whether to act in defense of the empire in the hands of a single official, the General Secretary. As long as those arrangements remained in force and that official was determined to maintain the empire, it stayed. When the time was right for that official to pull the props, the empire collapsed. The collapse came as a surprise because policymakers and specialists spent their time thinking about the Soviet Union as an international competitor, not about the possibility that Gorbachev might want the empire to disappear.

Chapter 5

Why Unemployment Benefits Have no Effect on Unemployment, but Unemployment Duration Does

George Tsebelis and Roland Stephen

The rise in unemployment during the 1970s and 1980s focused the attention of academics and policymakers on the level of unemployment benefits. What they discovered puzzled them. According to most economic models the level of unemployment benefit *causes* unemployment (Johnson and Layard 1986). The argument is that high benefits make the unemployed less willing to accept a job, and the employed more willing to quit their job. However, the empirical evidence connecting level of benefits with unemployment is quite weak (Atkinson et al. 1984; Narendranathan et al. 1985; Micklewright 1985). For example, countries like Germany and Sweden, with relatively high benefits (that is a high replacement rate of average production worker earnings), have enjoyed unemployment rates significantly below the OECD average (OECD 1990). A recent OECD study (1991a, 208) argues that "although different indicators could be used, it seems unlikely that this would result in any strong general cross-country correlation between benefit levels and unemployment rates emerging."

On the other hand, there is evidence of the dependence of unemployment on the duration of benefits. For example, Katz and Meyer (1990) find that in the United States entries into new jobs become more likely in the week before benefits terminate. In Japan, where benefit duration varies with age, Mizuno (1989) finds that exiting unemployment for each age group peaks around the period of benefit termination. The OECD (1991a, 207) study noted above claims that "labor market policies, or limited benefit duration or some combination of the two, are often an important factor in countries that have low levels of long-term unemployment."

The purpose of this chapter is to solve the mystery of why unemployment does not depend on the size of benefits, but on their duration. Moreover, we point out some of the simplifications in the theoretical economic literature that lead to the expectation that the size of benefits affects unemployment. Finally, we show that the size of benefits affects the level of monitoring of these benefits.

In a nutshell, the argument of the chapter is that most of the theoretical economic literature has ignored the institutional structure governing the administration of unemployment benefits. We present a model introducing such a structure. In particular, the model considers unemployment not as the aggregate outcome of the individual decisions of people entering and exiting two pools of employment and unemployment, but as a game between these people and employment agencies. In other words, unemployment in this paper is not considered as the isolated decision of a rational player, but as a game between two rational players. Consequently, how benefits are administered is as important as (or maybe more important than) the level of benefits.

The chapter is organized in three sections. Section 1 presents a review of the theoretical and empirical literature on unemployment benefits and their effects. With rare exceptions, institutional structures and monitoring have been ignored by the literature. Section 2 presents a simplified monitoring game between the unemployed and the employment agency. The agency helps the unemployed find a new job, but it may refuse benefits if reasonable work opportunities are rejected by the unemployed. This model yields the expectation that size of benefits has no effect on aggregate rates of unemployment, while the duration of benefits does have such an effect; moreover, the size of the benefits affects the intensity of monitoring. Section 3 presents historical empirical evidence in favor of the model from different European countries and tests its predictions cross-nationally with OECD data.

1.   Unemployment Benefits and Unemployment

In a review of different explanations for the natural level of unemployment in the *Handbook of Labor Economics,* Johnson and Layard (1986, 923) observe that "there has been an astonishing growth" of unemployment in Europe over the last fifteen years. They then present a series of models of the natural rate of unemployment. In all these models "unemployment insurance will increase unemployment" (923). They argue that these models "may also help to explain why unemployment has risen in countries where the replacement rate [the ratio of unemployment benefits to net income in work] has risen, or benefits become less painful to acquire" (924).

Similarly, Lippman and McCall (1979) and Hey (1979, chap. 14) consider job search models and demonstrate that an increase in unemployment benefits increases the probability that an unemployed person will remain unemployed. The argument is simple: The optimal search strategy for each unemployed person is to set a reservation wage w^*, follow the rule according to which he/she continues searching when receiving an offer lower than w^*, and accept any offer greater than w^*. In a search model, the greater w^* and the lower the search costs, the longer the time spend searching (and in the aggregate, the higher the unemployment level). Lippman and McCall (1979, 5) argue that "one of the predictions of the standard model is that the presence of unemployment insurance should increase . . . the duration of search [because] of the negative relationship between the cost of search and its expected duration." Finally, Atkinson et al. (1984, 3) start their paper with the following quotation from the economics literature, which, they argue, aptly summarizes the prevailing economic wisdom: "The theory of job search suggests that subsidized benefits of a general unemployment insurance system . . . create substitution effects in favor of greater frequency and longer duration periods of unemployment."

Atkinson and Micklewright (1991) review the unemployment benefits literature and report extensively on its assumptions and findings. This section is based to a large extent on their reports. They argue that there is a series of underlying assumptions in the standard economic literature:

> Unemployment benefit . . . is of the following "hypothetical form,"
> (a) the benefit is paid irrespective of the reasons for entry into
>   unemployment,
> (b) it is paid for all days of unemployment, from the onset of a spell,
> (c) it is independent of the person's efforts to search for new
>   employment, or of his or her availability for work,
> (d) there is no penalty to the refusal of job offers,
> (e) there are no contribution conditions related to past employment record
> (f) the benefit is paid at a flat rate
> (g) benefit is paid for an unlimited duration
> (h) eligibility for benefit is not affected by the level of income of other
>   household members. (1991, 1688)

However, in OECD countries unemployment benefits are refused when a person enters unemployment voluntarily or as a result of misconduct; they are in some cases not paid for an initial period; they are conditional upon genuine efforts to search for a new job; and they are withheld if the unemployed refuses to accept some specified number of "suitable" job offers. Consequently assumptions (a) to (d) are never met.

Moreover, OECD studies distinguish between unemployment insurance and unemployment assistance. Unemployment insurance is conditional either on past contributions or past record of insured employment; the benefits depend on past earnings; and the benefits are of limited duration and/or may decline over time. Consequently, unemployment insurance violates assumptions (e), (f), and (g) in addition to assumptions (a) through (d). Unemployment assistance on the other hand does not depend on previous contributions and is often of unlimited duration, but it may be means-tested not only with respect to the individual, but also with respect to other members of the household. Consequently, unemployment assistance in addition to violating (a) through (d) often violates assumptions (f) and (h).[1] However, the OECD (1988, 116) notes that even a simple classification of benefit schemes into insurance or assistance "types" is schematic and "useful only to a limited extent." A detailed examination of each country's scheme will indicate that classifying them into one category or another is rarely justified. The situation becomes more complicated by the fact that unemployment schemes differ "not only from one country to another, but also within each country" (OECD 1988, 119).

This account suggests that OECD countries do not provide unemployment benefits unconditionally. Instead they impose a series of restrictions, conditions, and tests. Moreover, they have a sizable mechanism to administer these tests. This monitoring mechanism takes the form of employment agencies. Their task is to screen unemployment claimants in order to see whether they meet the appropriate conditions, assist them in finding new employment, and reintegrate them into society. Very often there is either a separate branch of the employment agency or an entirely separate institution to provide training and job-search skills to the unemployed in order to accelerate their reintegration into the work force. Sometimes the payment of benefits is conditional upon the recipients accepting positions in educational or other training programs (this is characterized as a form of "workfare"). This is true of countries as diverse as Britain, Sweden, the United States, and Germany (see below for a discussion of all except the U.S. case).

However, all these structures may not adequately or effectively perform their declared functions, and it may well be that upon close examination the unemployment system of a country is adequately summarized by the size of the benefit. Even better, the conditions imposed on the recipients of unemployment benefits may be effective deterrents which prevent the undeserving unemployed from applying for them. If one of these assumptions were true all applicants would receive unemployment benefits: either because the monitoring mechanisms do not screen people, or because all frivolous applications are deterred.

A closer look at OECD countries indicates that this is not the case. The conditions of unemployment benefits are applied, and people are indeed screened out by employment offices. For example, a recent paper by Micklewright (1990) is entitled "Why Do Less than a Quarter of the Unemployed in Britain Receive Unemployment Insurance?" Blank and Card (1989) estimated that less than a third of the unemployed in the United States received unemployment insurance.[2] The major reasons for disqualification according to the U.S. Department of Health and Human Services (1989, 21) are voluntary separation, discharge for misconduct, refusal to apply or accept suitable work, or involvement in a labor dispute. In West Germany the percentage of unemployed that receive unemployment insurance is higher than in the United States and United Kingdom, but not by much: Brunhes and Annandale-Massa (1986) report that only 40 percent of those eligible received it in December of 1988. Finally, in Sweden, while the percentage of the unemployed receiving some kind of benefit is substantial, nearly 30 to 40 percent do not receive the benefit in the form of unemployment insurance payments (Bjorklund and Holmlund 1989, 169).

Further research indicates that the unemployed are dropped out not only from the more restrictive unemployment insurance schemes, but also from the more universal unemployment assistance programs. The number of unemployment claimants not receiving any form of assistance in the 1980s was around 20 percent in the United Kingdom and 30 percent in Germany (Atkinson and Micklewright 1991, 1693).

This brief and necessarily eclectic description indicates that the standard account of unemployment benefit as "the wage when not working" is an oversimplification of the situation, and that the institutional features of administering unemployment benefits, as well as the monitoring of the unemployment benefit claimants, have to be taken into consideration.

Now let us turn to the empirical side of the problem. Is it true that the level of unemployment benefits causes unemployment? In the beginning of the 1980s it seemed that the positive effect of benefits on unemployment was being confirmed in the empirical literature on the United Kingdom and the United States. Danziger et al. (1981, 992) reviewing the empirical economic literature for the United States came to the conclusion that "despite the problems, a positive relation between unemployment insurance and duration of unemployment appears robust." Lancaster and Nickell (1980) came to similar conclusions from their separate work on the United Kingdom. However, five years later the conclusions of literature reviews were quite different: Narendranathan et al. (1985, 307) report that "the diversity [of findings] has increased to the extent that estimates [of the elasticity of unemployment with respect to benefits] may now be found anywhere from negative to four."

In all these studies the size of the impact of benefits is quite small. For example, Lancaster and Nickell (1980) find that a 10 percent rise in benefits would increase the duration of unemployment by one week for a 17-week spell of unemployment. The American literature comes to similar conclusions. More recent work in the United States and the United Kingdom finds even smaller effects. For example Narendranathan et al. (1985) find a .3 elasticity of duration of unemployment (a 10 percent increase in benefit adds one week to a 33-week period of unemployment). Moffitt (1985) reports a .4 elasticity of duration of unemployment (a 10 percent increase in benefit extends a stretch of unemployment from 25 weeks to 26).

All these studies assume a constant probability for the transition from unemployment across different groups and across time. When econometric models allow for variable coefficients, it turns out that in the United Kingdom the benefit effect exists for teenagers but practically disappears after the age of twenty-five (Narendranathan et al. 1985). In different countries the effects vary across time. For example, the effects of benefits on the probability of exiting unemployment is positive and then zero in the United Kingdom (Nickell 1979a, b), while in Holland the effect increases after two years (van den Berg 1990).

More to the point, Atkinson et al. (1984) and Atkinson and Micklewright (1985) reanalyzed the U.K. data and found that when actual instead of nominal benefits are used as the independent variable (including changes of benefits over the period of unemployment), "the effect ceased to be significantly different from zero" (Atkinson and Micklewright 1991, 1711).

In other OECD countries Atkinson and Micklewright (1991, 1712) report that the effects of benefits on unemployment duration are also small or imprecise. Florens et al. (1990a, 342) find "ambiguous" effects from French data. Wurzel (1988) finds a negative but nonsignificant effect for West Germany, while Hujer and Schneider (1989) find that a switch from unemployment insurance to unemployment assistance (which implies a significant reduction in benefits) results in a significant fall in exit probability (the opposite of the expected effect). Ham and Rea (1987) find no significant effect with Canadian data, while Trivedi and Kapuscinski (1985) find robust but small effects.

The effects of unemployment benefits become even more ambiguous if one separates transitions from unemployment into different kinds of employment or exit from the labor market. For example, Clark and Summers (1982) find insignificant effects of benefits on transition to both employment and inactivity, while Barron and Mellow (1981) find that both effects are negative. In France, studies distinguishing among precarious and regular employment find a highly negative and significant effect of benefit size on transition to precarious jobs, and a less significant or insignificant effect on regular jobs (Atkinson and Micklewright 1991, 1714).

In contrast to the size of unemployment benefits, the duration of unemployment benefits seems to have clearer results. In country after country the typical result is that there is an increase in exit from unemployment right around the period of exhaustion of benefits. Here is OECD's (1991a, 207) account of the phenomenon: "In statistics for unemployed people with benefit entitlements of a specific duration, monthly rates of exit from unemployment seem typically to decline in the first month or several months of unemployment, rise before benefit exhaustion, and reach peak levels in the month or several months after exhaustion, before falling back again." OECD's evidence comes from France (Florens et al. 1990b), from Canada (Ham and Rea 1987), from Spain (Alba-Ramirez and Freeman 1990), and from Japan (Mizuno 1989). Similar effects for the United States can be found in Moffitt and Nicholson 1982 and Moffitt 1985. Some studies find opposite patterns (increased probability of exiting unemployment as a function of time) for particular, country-specific reasons. For example, Bjorklund (1990) finds such a relationship in Sweden and hypothesizes that it is caused by particular attention paid by unemployment offices to the placement of long-term unemployed. Andersen (1989) explains a similar pattern in Holland by the existence of government-sponsored temporary work programs offered to people whose entitlement was near its end.

Katz and Meyer (1990), analyzing U.S. data, find that a change in unemployment benefit duration has more impact than a change in unemployment benefit level, and through simulations they come to the conclusion that a cut in unemployment insurance is twice as efficient if it affects the duration of unemployment benefits rather than the level. Moreover, they find that the probability of unemployment ending is higher when a claimant would reasonably expect benefits to be terminated, even if they are extended.

To recapitulate, the standard result of positive association between level of unemployment benefits and unemployment provided by economists is based on assumptions that do not approximate the conditions prevailing in OECD countries. The theoretical result is derived because institutional structures regulating the administration of such benefits are ignored. In addition, the monitoring of these benefits is completely left aside. Starting from the empirical side of the question we are led to similar results: empirical evidence in favor of an association between unemployment benefits and unemployment is weak. On the contrary, there is evidence linking duration of unemployment benefits with duration of unemployment. In the next part, we present a model linking the institutional structures and administration of unemployment benefits, and in particular monitoring by employment agencies, with levels of unemployment. This model presents comparative statics consistent with the empirical findings.

2.   Monitoring Unemployment Benefits.

Consider the interaction between the unemployed and the unemployment agency. The unemployed presents a claim that he or she fulfills the requirements for unemployment compensation. Such requirements are most of the below: that the person did not quit the job voluntarily or as a result of misconduct; that he or she has not been working part time; that he or she makes genuine efforts to find work, or that he or she is available for work, and willing to accept a job if one is offered; that their previous employment paid the necessary contributions into an unemployment insurance fund; that they pass a means test. After receiving such a petition the unemployment agency checks whether the claims are correct, then either pays or withholds the appropriate amount. Now this interaction may be repeated over time, in order to verify that the status of the individual claimant has not changed, or, in the event that unemployment lasts for a long period, to move a person from unemployment insurance to unemployment assistance. As was made clear in section 1, not all persons apply for unemployment benefits, and of those who do apply some are refused because they do not qualify. Because the interaction of agency and unemployed occurs over time, so does the process of disqualification. A person initially offered unemployment benefits may be dropped subsequently from the list (because, for example, he or she was offered a job several times and did not accept it). Conversely, a person initially disqualified can be reinstated, because of an appeal process or because the period of disqualification has ended.

We will simplify this process by considering it as a one-shot interaction. We will divide the population of unemployed into "meritorious" and "nonmeritorious." The first group is one that fulfills all the requirements of the unemployment compensation system of a given country, while the second is one which lacks at least one of the required qualifications and therefore is not entitled to unemployment benefits according to the law. We want to investigate whether this nonmeritorious category gets artificially inflated by increases in benefits, that is, whether more generous benefits increase the numbers of claimants who are nonmeritorious because they provide incentives to this group to exit employment and claim, or to refuse offers of employment and claim.

The difference between the meritorious and nonmeritorious people is that the first will apply more frequently, since they have nothing to lose from scrutiny of their application, while the second will apply only if they think there is a reasonable chance that they will be granted the benefits. We will distinguish two cases: In the first (and simpler) story, the meritorious will have a dominant strategy to apply. In the second, the meritorious will not have such a dominant strategy, and they will be deterred by a "sufficiently high" frequency of scrutiny by the agency. We include this second story because there are accounts indicating that even meritorious people sometimes do not apply for benefits because of lack of information, or because they are deterred by means tests, or because of other transaction costs (Atkinson and Micklewright 1991, 1693–94). The appendix will demonstrate that the two stories lead to identical outcomes, so the narrative (in this section) will follow only the first.

The agency has the task of investigating whether a particular claim comes from a meritorious person and grant it, or a nonmeritorious person and reject it. The game is presented in figure 1. In this game, a person is meritorious (with probability x) or nonmeritorious (with probability $(1 - x)$).[3] Then, the person has the choice of making an application to the unemployment agency. Finally, if an application is made, the agency decides whether to scrutinize it or not. If it scrutinizes, it will grant the applications of meritorious people and reject the applications of nonmeritorious people. If it does not scrutinize, it will grant all applications automatically.

Let us focus on the incentives of the agency. If all people were meritorious it would prefer to grant all claims without scrutiny. If, however, the percentage of nonmeritorious claimants is high, then the agency has to step up the monitoring efforts in order to screen people more effectively. Note that this account of the agency seems to ignore other players in the game, such as elected politicians who instruct the agency how to behave, or the electorate who may be more or less sensitive to arguments about the overwhelming public expenses of the unemployed.[4] This impression is incorrect. Changes in the political environment will be reflected in the agency's payoffs. For example, "turning the screw" will be reflected on higher disutility for the agency if nonmeritorious applicants receive unemployment benefits.

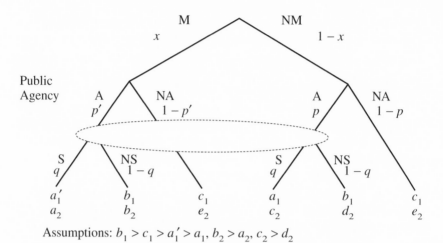

Assumptions: $b_1 > c_1 > a'_1 > a_1, b_2 > a_2, c_2 > d_2$

Figure 1. Unemployment benefit monitoring game. (M = meritorious; NM = not meritorious; A = apply; NA = not apply; S = scrutinize; NS = not scrutinize.)

Formally, the assumptions can be presented by the following inequalities of the payoffs of the different players.

Assumption 1:   The nonmeritorious unemployed prefer to apply when they will not be scrutinized, and not to apply when they will be scrutinized. Formally: $b_1 > c_1 > a_1$

Assumption 2:   The meritorious unemployed prefer to apply.[5]

Assumption 3:   The agency prefers to scrutinize nonmeritorious applicants, and not to scrutinize meritorious ones. Formally: $b_2 > a_2$

Under assumptions 1, 2, and 3, the nonmeritorious unemployed will apply if they will not be scrutinized and the probability of being caught and stigmatized is low. Similarly, the agency will try to keep scrutiny at levels high enough to deter the nonmeritorious from applying. But where are these thresholds?

The calculations of the equilibrium strategies of the two actors are presented in the appendix. These calculations indicate that the nonmeritorious will always apply with some positive probability. This probability is calculated to be:

$$p^* = (x(b_2 - a_2))/((1 - x)(c_2 - d_2)) \tag{1}$$

Equation (1) indicates that when the proportion of meritorious applicants is high, then all the nonmeritorious unemployed will apply. In fact:

$$\text{if } x \geq (c_2 - d_2)/(b_2 - a_2 + c_2 - d_2), \text{ then } p^* = 1 \tag{2}$$

On the other hand, the agency, once it receives an application, believes it comes from a meritorious applicant with probability

$$p(M/A) = ((1 - x)p)/((x + (1 - x)p) \tag{3}$$

As a consequence, the agency will scrutinize with frequency

$$q^* = (b_1 - c_1)/(b_1 - a_1) \tag{4}$$

Equations (1) to (4) describe the equilibrium strategies of the players in the unemployment monitoring game. We can use them to investigate the consequences of a series of modifications in the administration of unemployment benefits. For example, what happens if one increases the size of the benefits, or the duration of the benefits, or the proportion of unemployed, or the composition of the unemployed (the ratio of meritorious to nonmeritorious) in the system?

Let us identify first the consequences of an increase in the unemployment benefit. How is a change in the unemployment benefit represented in our model? Such a change is reflected by the amount b_1 the applicants receive. However, this payoff does not figure as a parameter in the equilibrium strategy of the unemployed (meritorious or nonmeritorious). These people do not apply with higher frequency when unemployment benefits increase. Equations (1) and (4) in our model indicate that an increase in unemployment benefits does not increase the proportion of nonmeritorious to meritorious applicants. Instead, an increase in benefits has, as a consequence, an increase in the scrutinizing frequency of the agency. Conversely, a decrease in benefits reduces monitoring of the unemployment agency.

This conclusion may seem implausible, but it is a standard result of two-person games with mixed strategy equilibria (Tsebelis 1989, 1990a; Bianco et al. 1990). Changes in the payoff of one actor are offset by modifications in the equilibrium strategy of the other actor. The reason is that in equilibrium both players are indifferent between their two pure strategies. So, in order to make the nonmeritorious applicants indifferent between applying and not applying, the unemployment agency increases its monitoring frequency.

Let us now investigate the consequences of a change in the payoffs of the agency. The logic developed above indicates that such changes will be reflected in the behavior of the unemployed. Indeed, if the political environment pressures the agency to keep a watchful eye, resulting in an increase in the payoffs a_2 and particularly c_2 (the payoff for discovering and rejecting non-meritorious applicants), the number of frivolous applications will go down. Consequently, changes in the payoff of monitoring for the unemployment agency will have an impact on unemployment.

One interesting application of this reasoning is the problem of workfare. Several governments (United Kingdom, United States, Sweden) provide un-employment benefits that are conditional upon enrollment in some educational or work-training program. What is the impact of such policies, according to our model? Workfare programs have trivial monitoring costs per se. Their over-all cost is very high because they require educational and administrative per-sonnel, but these people do not have to investigate whether the participants are meritorious or not. Participation in the program is equivalent to merit. The program design contains a built-in monitoring mechanism without any further specific action by agency officials. Consequently, cheating goes to zero accord-ing to our model.

King and Ward (1992) have made the claim that traditional unemployment benefit programs create pooling equilibria where "all unemployed people will claim" and that workfare schemes generate a "partial separating equilibrium under which some claimants identified by the state as undeserving are dis-couraged from seeking benefits." While the intuition that workfare reduces cheating is correct, King and Ward (1992) fail to identify the mechanism by which the result is obtained. In their model all strategic interactions between monitoring and monitored are ignored and replaced by exogenously given probabilities. Consequently, according to their model, traditional unemploy-ment benefit programs do not have any built-in deterrent, while the deterrent of workfare programs is that participants have to work. But if both meritorious and nonmeritorious apply in traditional programs, as they imply, either there would be no disqualifications (if there is no monitoring) or disqualifications would be much higher (if there is monitoring). Since monitoring is absent in their model, variations in the level of benefits would result in variations in the level of unemployment, exactly as in the economic models reviewed in the first section of this study.

Our model predicts that deterrent mechanisms resulting from monitoring exist both in traditional unemployment programs and in workfare programs. The difference is that the payoffs of the monitoring agency differ systemati-cally (monitoring is built-in in workfare), and consequently they lead to different aggregate levels of cheating. And while workfare in the King and Ward (1992) article characterizes right-wing governments exclusively, in our model there are two different reasons for adopting the same kind of program: either the goal is to reduce cheating (a "right-wing" reason) or the goal is to train workers for a constantly changing economic environment (a "left-wing" reason).[6]

Suppose now that the total number of unemployed increases. The simplest assumption is that such an increase, by itself, will not modify the proportion (x) of meritorious people in the pool. We will investigate the consequences under this assumption and discuss changes in x in the next paragraph. If unemployment rises and x remains unchanged, the payoffs of the agency are changed since scrutiny becomes more difficult. As a consequence the number of frivolous applications increases.

Suppose that the proportion of the meritorious unemployed (x) decreases. This modification of x has no consequence on the monitoring behavior of the agency. It is the equilibrium strategy of the nonmeritorious unemployed that is affected. The number of frivolous applications goes down, so that the percentage of frivolous to nonfrivolous *applications* remains the same. In fact, the ratio $x/(1 - x)p^*$ remains constant,[7] except when the percentage of meritorious unemployed is so high that all nonmeritorious unemployed find it profitable to apply (a so-called corner solution).

Our conclusions sharply contrast with the search models in economics. They argue that an increase in unemployment benefits decreases search costs and consequently increases the length of search for all unemployed, which in turn increases the rate of unemployment. We argue that the introduction of a monitoring agency alters this result in a dramatic way. First, modifications of the payoffs of the unemployed get absorbed by the behavior of the agency. Second, even modifications in the composition of the unemployed (which may result from a change in benefits) are absorbed by changes in their behavior, since when the number of the nonmeritorious increases, they apply less frequently.

The comparative statics of this model can help us make a series of predictions about unemployment benefits and their consequences on unemployment. As we explained, according to our model, the size of unemployment benefits has no effect on unemployment but increases monitoring. Consequently, if we apply our reasoning to different countries we would expect that

- countries with high benefits do not have different unemployment levels from countries with low unemployment benefits;
- countries with high benefits will have a more developed monitoring apparatus.

Application of the same model in cross-country comparisons indicates that a change in the duration of unemployment benefits will not affect the behavior of people: meritorious and nonmeritorious unemployed will continue applying at the same proportion. But while the number of unemployed at any period of time will not be affected, these people will remain in the public payroll for longer periods of time, so the aggregate unemployment level will rise. In other words:

- countries with long duration of unemployment benefits will have high levels of unemployment.

Finally, since in periods of high unemployment the nonmeritorious unemployed increase the number of their applications, while the agency continues monitoring at the same rate, the number of rejections will increase disproportionately. So,

- In periods of high unemployment, rejections of unemployment applications increase disproportionately.

In the next section we test these propositions empirically.

3. Monitoring Unemployment Benefits
    in Comparative Perspective

The model in the previous section provides propositions that can be tested both over time and cross-nationally. For empirical tests we divide this section into two parts. In the first part we draw on experiences of seven OECD countries over the last two decades that prove to be consistent with our model. In the second section we present cross-national comparisons with OECD data.

Each of these sections presents significant shortcomings. The interpretation of illustrative evidence taken from the historical experiences of a group of countries naturally focuses on experiences that are congruent with our model. There may be other plausible explanations that account for some of them. However, we know of no other theory that accounts for all the evidence presented in the case studies as well for all the cross-national comparisons we present in the two parts of this section. The cross-national comparisons are more systematic but, like any regression model, are based on the unrealistic assumption that the different countries come from the same distribution. We will address this assumption below.

We rejected a pooled time-series analysis for two reasons. The first is that the main time-series required for our model (that is, variations in the size of monitoring mechanisms) does not exist for any country. The second is that even if such time-series existed, increased monitoring does not necessarily translate immediately into an increase in the number of inspectors in the unemployment agency. Consequently, without having a model of government reaction to agency insufficiencies, we can only test the proposition that increased unemployment benefits will cause increased monitoring on the average.

Case Studies

In this section we will sketch the recent experience of seven OECD countries (Sweden, Ireland, Canada, Britain, Germany, France, Australia). These countries were chosen because they represent a rich series of contrasts along significant dimensions: for example, the role of insurance versus assistance, the budgetary constraints faced by each government, the level of unemployment, and the different policy changes experienced.

Sweden

In Sweden benefits are generous by the standards of other countries. The initial gross replacement rate of unemployment benefits for a single person is 90 percent, the highest of all OECD countries (OECD 1991a, 201). Supervision of the unemployed is also high. There is one staff person in the unemployment offices for every 14 unemployed, which is the lowest ratio in all OECD countries (213). The relationship between high benefits and high levels of monitoring seems to be confirmed, at least, by this limiting case.

There was a significant rise in the real value of benefits in the late 1970s and early 1980s. Bjorklund and Holmlund (1989) established, as noted, that there seemed to be no benefit-induced unemployment. Our model suggests that we would see an increase in monitoring in conjunction with this rise in real benefits, and in fact, following a 1979 report, there was an increase in the number of Labor Market Board (AMS) personnel allocated to placement activities (Standing 1988, 109).

Active labor market expenditures changed in character at the same time, from increasing the efficiency and flexibility of the labor market to the use of subsidies to keep people in jobs or public works, and therefore out of the job market (Standing 1988, 113). For these workers the government avoided play-ing the monitoring game.

Youth unemployment was addressed with a combination of both monitor-ing and government job creation. This had the effect of limiting their access to benefits. A report from the Ministry of Labor remarked, "The right of 18–19 year olds to a youth team job replaces their rights to unemployment benefits" (Standing 1988, 111). The role of monitoring and workfare programs seems to be especially significant for this group in all countries that we examine.

In conclusion, Sweden is generous in benefits and monitors them closely, while also using job subsidies and job training. These other strategies (among other things) limit the need to monitor. By 1985, while the "open" unemploy-ment rate was 3 percent, a further 3.5 percent of those employed were in labor market schemes (Standing 1988, 107).

Ireland

Unemployment in this country has been persistently the highest among OECD countries, nearly twice that of the OECD average, and between 1980 and 1988 it more than doubled (OECD 1991b, 43). This had two consequences. By 1989 total unemployment benefits, combined with the cost of the Training and Em-ployment Authority (FAS), was about 4.8 percent of GNP. This severe fiscal constraint was relieved only by contributions from the EC.

The second consequence was increased cheating. Notwithstanding the fiscal difficulties, the Irish government increased monitoring and job creation (remember always that monitoring is costly compared, for example, to low levels of benefits paid permissively). In 1986 an External Control Unit was added to an existing Special Investigation Unit, signaling the increase in mon-itoring. About 7,000 initial claims for unemployment benefits were rejected in 1989, about 7 percent of total applications (DSW 1990, 78). A training pro-gram was established by the Labor Services Act, 1987, and refusal of a place in these schemes was grounds for loss of benefits (DSW 1988, 75). Young people in particular had to be engaged in a training program or involved in so-cial employment.

To sum up, Ireland, a country with relatively low benefits (OECD 1991a, 201), faced a double difficulty in the 1980s: overwhelming levels of unem-ployment and severe fiscal constraints. Despite low benefits, monitoring was increased and workfare-type programs instituted because, we suggest, the non-meritorious had a dominant strategy to cheat as a result of the presence of so many meritorious in the pool of unemployed. The government also attempted to move people out of the monitoring game altogether using job creation.

Canada

This country has an unemployment benefits system based on the insurance principle only. The first oil shock caused a jump in unemployment; between 1974 and 1979 it averaged 7.2 percent (OECD 1991b, 43). One response was to increase monitoring through the regulatory powers of the Unemployment Insurance Commission. The number of benefit control officers was doubled, and the number disqualified each month rose from 9.1 to 14.5 percent between 1972 and 1974. In 1975 new rules on registration, interviews, and employment records were instituted (Pal 1988, 45). This confirms our proposition that disqualifications increase disproportionately under circumstances of rising unemployment.

Canada pursues a "permissive" entitlement strategy. The result is that generous payments and low levels of monitoring make the incentive to work and claim low. The problem of those who claim without seeking work might be overlooked because the duration of Canada's benefits is low in comparison with all other OECD countries (OECD 1991a, 201). A time limit on benefits, rather than supervision of the clients, is Canada's strategy in response to the monitoring problem.

In conclusion, a rise in unemployment was accompanied by a disproportionate rise in disqualifications, as predicted by our model. Paying benefits for a short period seems to be an alternative to the difficulties, and expense, of monitoring.

Britain

The new Conservative government in 1979 believed that there was insurance-induced unemployment (Brown 1990, 51). Therefore a variety of policies were introduced that had the overall effect of lowering benefits. Cost-of-living increases in Unemployment Benefit (UB) were restricted, Earnings Related Supplement (ERS) and dependent child payments eliminated, and the qualification requirements stiffened. This seems to be a strategy of simple cuts in benefits, rather than choosing a conditional (and expensive) welfare game. This is congruent with our model: low benefits are accompanied by low levels of monitoring.

Atkinson and Micklewright (1989, 23) note that the real level of the UB had recovered by 1984 and had improved slightly by 1985, before falling back to 1979 levels by 1987. It was at the point when benefits started to rise, following the Social Security review of 1984, that there was a change in strategy by the British government toward a policy of monitoring. This accords with our model: large numbers of unemployed and low levels of monitoring resulted in a dominant strategy for the nonmeritorious to "cheat." As benefits rose, so too did the importance of monitoring.[8] A different story, also consistent with our model, is that monitoring was low because the nonmeritorious had been deterred by the increased interest of the Conservative government in catching them. But this is not consistent with the following report of the National Audit Office: In 1985 the National Audit Office criticized Unemployment Review Officers for failing to adequately review the claims submitted for benefits. There were about 100 officers in the 1970s; by 1988 their numbers had been increased to 796. A wide range of other changes were made that included new and more exhaustive questionnaires for the unemployed, weekly self-reporting, increased penalties for voluntary dismissal, interviews, tightened work availability rules, and a new category of monitors for the newly unemployed, New Client Advisers. Disallowance of benefits rose from 39,000 in 1981 to 101,000 in 1987, which confirms our prediction that disqualifications rise during periods of high unemployment (Brown 1990, 178–203).

In summary the British experience in the recent past shows a range of policy responses. Lower benefits and lower monitoring were followed by a change in course in which monitoring was increased due to the combination of a rise in real benefits and an easing of the fiscal constraints on the government; in addition, disqualifications rose as unemployment rose, as our model suggests.

Germany

In Germany all benefits to the unemployed are part of a larger, fully integrated set of active labor market policies. The benefits are a fairly high percentage of previous wages, between 58 and 63 percent (ILO 1986, 114). As our model would predict, the Federal Republic monitors those claiming benefits fairly closely. The Federal Labor Office has wide powers to promote certain trades, as well as powers to direct and constrain beneficiaries (Kerschen and Kessler 1990, 276–77).

Germany too faced the challenge of increased unemployment in the late 1970s and early 1980s: the rate rose from 3.3 percent in 1979 to 8.0 percent in 1985 (OECD 1991b, 43). This resulted in increased monitoring, which attracted significant political debate. In 1982 there were changes made in the availability rule in which work further from home was now considered acceptable, and in which work not commensurate with a person's skills had to be accepted after a reduced grace period (Karasch 1983, 70–71). In fact disqualifications rose throughout the decade; there were 18,000 in 1984 and 36,000 in 1989 (BAS 1990, 30–31). In Germany too increased unemployment resulted in increased monitoring and increased disqualifications.

France

While unemployment insurance payments have been generous in France in the past, in the late 1970s they amounted to as much as 90 percent of previous earnings, and in 1991 they declined to 60 percent (OECD 1991a, 201). After all allowances are exhausted there is a sharp drop in level of benefits, which are paid as a form of general assistance (which is indefinite in duration, except for those under 25) (ILO 1986, 117). The government in France avoids the monitoring game, it seems, by paying high levels of benefits to the short-term unemployed, but very low levels of benefits to the long-term and youth unemployed. The prospect of the sharp decline in benefits has the effect of increasing the intensity of the job search, as noted by the OECD (1991a, 206) and Florens et al. (1990a).

The French government resorted to other strategies that kept people out of the monitoring game in response to the high levels of unemployment in the 1980s. Between 1982 and 1983 the money spent on promoting early retirement rose from 28 to 50 billion francs per annum (SES 1986, 404). By this means many older workers were taken off the unemployment rolls. Job subsidies, "enterprise" allowances, and shortened working hours were also used to keep people out of the ranks of the officially unemployed.

Another interesting aspect of the French system is the way costs, such as the costs of training, are imposed on private sector employers (SES 1986, 179). This reflects a pattern of policy-making in which administrative responsibilities and costs are minimized or shared with other actors.

In the face of high unemployment and a crisis in finance of the unemployment system, France lowered benefits and pursued other strategies designed to avoid costly monitoring. While we have an explanation for the way benefits and monitoring are related, it is important to remember that we do not claim to account for the level of benefits—in part, in the French case among others, this may be a function of institutional capacity (as is discussed further below).

Australia

This country historically has paid low levels of benefits permissively, that is, with low monitoring. In 1983 unemployment jumped to almost 10 percent and remained stubbornly high for the next five years. The Australian system had a limited capacity to monitor, therefore cheating became a dominant strategy for the nonmeritorious. In order to move the nonmeritorious off this corner solution, we would expect an expansion of the monitoring apparatus, even though benefits were low (q^*, the likelihood of the agency scrutinizing, rises if the probability of payoff c_1 to the nonmeritorious, the payoff for not applying, becomes zero). In keeping with this there was a radical departure in monitoring in 1986 with the establishment of mobile review teams, in combination with an intensified program of general reviews by regional office staff. The result in 1989–90 was over 25,000 disqualifications of unemployment beneficiaries (DSS 1990, 111). These disqualifications were the direct result of a new emphasis on monitoring (109).

Conclusion

Our core proposition is that high benefits require high levels of monitoring. The rise in benefits in Sweden and the decline in benefits (at first) in Britain were accompanied by the appropriate rise and decline in monitoring. In periods of high unemployment, disqualifications increased in Canada, Germany, Britain, and Australia, as our model also predicts. Although small changes in the propensity to cheat by the nonmeritorious leave the equilibrium level of cheating unchanged in our model, we identify several instances in which the lack of monitoring combined with high unemployment has caused these nonmeritorious to pursue a dominant strategy. This has resulted in an expansion of the monitoring capacity by the governments involved, in spite of a low level of benefits. We have also observed how monitoring is avoided by adopting alternative strategies, and the special interest of all countries in the training, education, and socialization of younger workers.

Cross-National Comparisons

Here we report a series of statistical results designed to test some of the predictions of our model, in particular those that could not be fruitfully examined in the descriptive section above. The underlying assumption of such a comparison is that the observations come from the same distribution. This assumption is violated because, as we pointed out, the institutional structures of unemployment benefit administration vary widely from country to country.

Let us discuss these differences in institutional structures further, because our argument is that the fit of our model (r^2) is low because of these differences. The objection might be raised that a systematic study of these differences would completely cancel out our findings. However, such an objection, to be sustained, requires such a (very welcome) systematic study. For the time being let us merely illustrate the differences that our empirical test will necessarily ignore.

In Canada the institutional autonomy of the Unemployment Insurance Commission, which played no part in active labor market measures (job training, etc.), did not end until it was amalgamated with the Department of Manpower and Immigration in 1975 (Pal 1988, 132). There have never been workfare-type programs, and the most recent commission to review unemployment policy, the Forget Commission in 1986, attempted to return the program to its "pure" insurance form and limit government subventions. The absence of monitoring is clearly partly the result of Canadian institutional arrangements.

Unemployment insurance is managed in France by the National Occupational Union for Employment in Industry and Commerce (UNEDIC) and a public sector counterpart, the Association for Employment in Industry and Commerce (ASSEDIC). These are private law institutions managed jointly by the peak associations of labor and capital. Entirely separate from this arrangement is the Ministère du Travail, de l'Emploi et de la Formation professionelle. It is this ministry which spent 11 billion francs on active labor market policies in 1983 (SES 1986, 177, 404). This institutional separation is also, we suggest, partly responsible for the low level of monitoring in France.

Let us turn now to empirical tests that rely on cross-national data supplied by the OECD (OECD 1990, 1991a, 1991b). The data are reproduced in table 1 and the results are listed in table 2. Many of the relationships we report are bivariate. The reason is that our purpose is to show that some significant relationship exists between, for example, monitoring and the level of benefits. We do not propose a comprehensive account, in which most of the significant variables are captured. For this purpose bivariate analysis is adequate, unless other variables exist that obviously confound the analysis. We attempt to identify such cases when they occur.

We began by regressing benefits against unemployment. Benefits are expressed as a proportion of an average production worker's wage in each country. This captures their "generosity" relative to the income level for each country. Unemployment is an eight-year average, in order to smooth away cyclical or stochastic economic factors. As reported on line 1 there seems to be a weak inverse relationship between benefits and unemployment, which is counter to the "common sense" view.

Inasmuch as benefits are a political choice, perhaps the problem with the "common sense" view (that high benefits induce unemployment) has less to do with the strategic interaction we examine and more to do with the fact that governments of the "left" prefer high levels of benefits and low levels of unemployment (and governments of the "right" the reverse). In that event we would expect a significant result from regressing a measure of left government and the level of benefits against unemployment (admitting beforehand the collinearity between the two variables).[9] As reported on line 2, neither variable appears to be significantly related to unemployment. In the case of left governments, the fact that we are dealing only with the 1980s, as opposed to whole postwar period, may explain the lack of a connection. We also regressed left

TABLE 1.   Variables Relating to Unemployment Benefits in Comparative Perspectives

County	[MONIT][a]	[BENEF][b]	[DURTN][c]	[UAVG][d]	[LFTGV][e]	[GVTEMP][f]
Australia	109	24	—	7.7	33.75	26.7
Austria	74	41	30	3.5	48.67	19.6
Belgium	—	60	—	11.2	43.25	20.4
Canada	213	60	50	9.7	0	19.9
Denmark	81	64	120	8.3	90.24	29.7
Finland	55	59	104	5.1	59.33	20.3
France	271	59	120	8.9	8.67	22.8
Germany	86	58	52	6.9	35.33	15.5
Greece	—	50	20	6.4	—	—
Ireland	733	29	60	13.8	0	15.9
Italy	—	15	24	9.5	0	15.2
Japan	—	48	30	2.5	1.92	6.4
Netherlands	152	70	144	10.1	31.5	16
New Zealand	175	27	—	—	60	18
Norway	68	62	80	2.4	83.08	25.2
Portugal	266	60	—	7.9	—	12.2
Spain	713	62	104	17.6	—	14.3
Sweden	14	90	60	2.7	111.8	32.6
Switzerland	15	70	50	0.7	11.87	11.2
Turkey	—	—	—	15.2	—	—
United Kingdom	53	16	52	10.1	43.67	21.8
United States	—	50	26	7.6	0	14.8

[a]A measure of the degree to which the unemployed are monitored, this is the average number of unemployed per staff person in the unemployment service. We inverted it (making it the fraction of a staff person per unemployed). Drawn from column 1, table 4, OECD 1990, 32.

[b]A measure of unemployment benefits expressed as a fraction of the salary of the average production worker in each country (Initial Gross Replacement Rate). Drawn from column 7, table 7.2, OECD 1991a, 201.

[c]A measure of the maximum duration of initial benefits in weeks, assuming that the unemployed satisfied the employment record requirement. Drawn from column 4, table 7.2, OECD 1991a, 201.

[d]Average unemployment for the period 1980–87, drawn from table 2.15, OECD 1991b, 43.

[e]An index of the history of left governments for a selection of countries, developed by Wilensky (1981). Each country is given from zero to three points for each year of leftist (Communist, Socialist, Social Democratic, etc.) participation in government, depending on their role in any governing coalition.

[f]Government employment as a percentage of total employment in 1985. This year was chosen as being the most recent year in which data is available for all OECD countries. Year-to-year change in this number tends to be incremental. Drawn from table 2.13, OECD 1992b, 42.

government against level of benefits, to check whether there was a relationship, and as reported in line 3 the connection is a weak one.

Since there is only a weak relationship between left governments and the level of benefits, it is not surprising that there is also only weak connection between left governments and monitoring, as reported in line 4. This is because a basic implication of our model is that high benefits lead to high levels of monitoring, not to high unemployment. This is examined directly in line 5,

TABLE 2.   The Relation between Unemployment, Benefits, and Monitoring

Dependent Variable	Independent Variable	Sign	Standard Beta	t-statistic (Corr.)	r^2	n
1. UAVGPAVG	BENEF	−	0.27	1.21	0.08	20
2. UAVGPAVG	BENEF	−	0.34	1.28	0.10	17
	LFTGV	−	0.19	0.73		
3. BENEF	LFTGVT	+	0.41	1.68	0.10	18
4. MONIT	LFTGVT	+	0.37	1.34	0.06	14
5. MONIT	BENEF	+	0.46	2.03	0.17	16
6. MONIT	LEFT	+	0.21	0.810	0.21	14
	BENEF	+	0.47	1.826		
7. UAVG	DURTN	+	0.32	1.30	0.04	17
8. MONIT	BENEF	+	0.44	1.92	0.15	16
	GVTEMP	+	0.19	0.77		

where a strong connection, confirming our model, is discovered (between benefits and monitoring). Left government and level of benefit are regressed together against level of monitoring in line 6, and benefits still prove to be significant, while the connection with left government remains a weak one (note that n is very low in this case).

With our next test, reported in line 7, we discovered a weak positive relationship between duration of benefits and unemployment, which the model also predicts. We were unable to find a measure of duration of benefits that captured changes in the rules over the eight-year period. While these changes may not be insignificant, we take the rules on duration reported in OECD 1991a as a reasonable proxy for the rules over a longer period.

To summarize, the "common sense" view of benefit-induced unemployment is not consistent with our data. Nor does there seem to be a strong relationship between left government, unemployment, or level of benefit. However, level of benefit does significantly influence the level of monitoring, as we argue.[10] Finally, the relationship between the duration of benefits and unemployment is weak but positive, as suggested by our model and the empirical findings of others.

Conclusion

The predominant economic approach on unemployment benefits summarizes the benefit policy of a country by the size of benefits and expects unemployment to increase with the size of benefits. Along with several economists (Atkinson and Micklewright 1991) we argued that the institutions regulating benefits should be introduced into the picture. Moreover, we argued that one important aspect of the question has been completely ignored by the literature: monitoring of unemployment benefits.

We proposed a simple monitoring game between unemployment agency and unemployed population. The conclusions of this game are very different from existing economic (see first part) or decision-theoretic (King and Ward 1992) approaches. In particular, the predictions of our model are consistent with a series of facts:

- The effect of unemployment benefits on unemployment is either non-existent, or very small. According to our crude cross-national data it is even negative.
- There is a cross-national moderate effect of duration of unemployment benefits on unemployment.
- The size of unemployment benefits affects the intensity of monitoring (size of unemployment agency).
- Countries with high participation of the Left in government monitor more than countries where the Right predominates.

APPENDIX

Part A

The meritorious have dominant strategy to apply. The reader is reminded of the assumptions from the text:

Assumption A1: $b_1 > c_1 > a_1$

Assumption A2:   Meritorious unemployed always apply.

Assumption A3: $b_2 > a_2, c_2 > d_2$

Assumption A4:   The proportion of meritorious is x.

Calculation of equilibrium strategies:

$$EU_{NA} = c_1 \tag{1A}$$

$$EU_A = qa_1 + (1 - q)b_1 \tag{2A}$$

The beliefs of the agency when they receive an application are given by Bayes's theorem.

$$p(M/A) = ((1 - x)p)/((x + (1 - x)p), \text{ and } p(NM/A) = 1 - p(M/A) \qquad (3A)$$

On the basis of these beliefs, the expected utilities of the agency's pure strategies are calculated as follows.

$$EU_S = xa_2 + (1 - x)pc_2 \qquad (4A)$$

$$EU_{NS} = xb_2 + (1 - x)pd_2 \qquad (5A)$$

In equilibrium each player is indifferent between his or her pure strategies. Setting the first two expected utilities equal to each other we get

$$q^* = (b_1 - c_1)/(b_1 - a_1) \qquad (6A)$$

Similarly, from (4A) and (5A) we get

$$p^* = (x(b_2 - a_2))/((1 - x)(c_2 - d_2)) \qquad (7A)$$

Equations (6A) and (7A) present the following situation: The monitoring agency will always monitor with a probability that depends on the payoffs of the monitored player. The monitored player will always cheat with some probability. However, under certain conditions cheating occurs with probability 1. From (7A),

$$\text{if } x \geq (c_2 - d_2)/(b_2 - a_2 + c_2 - d_2), \text{ then } p^* = 1 \qquad (8A)$$

Part B

The meritorious do not have a dominant strategy.

Assumption A1: $b_1 > c_1 > a_1$

Assumption A2': $b_1 > c_1 > a_1'$ (with $a_1' > a_1$)

Assumption A3: $b_2 > a_2, c_2 > d_2$

Assumption A4:   The proportion of meritorious is x.

From assumption A2' follows that meritorious and nonmeritorious cannot be indifferent between applying and not applying at the same time (for the same frequency of scrutiny). In addition, nonmeritorious are more deterrable than meritorious. Consequently, there are two candidates for equilibrium, Equilibrium 1: All meritorious apply, and nonmeritorious mix, and Equilibrium 2: All nonmeritorious do not apply, and meritorious mix.

It is easy to see that Equilibrium 1 is identical to the equilibrium calculated in part A. Moreover, it is easy to demonstrate that Equilibrium 2 does not exist: Indeed, if the frequency of scrutiny is so high as to deter the nonmeritorious, every applicant would be a meritorious one, in which case the agency would not scrutinize at all. Consequently, under assumptions A1, A2', A3, and A4 the only equilibrium is identical with the one calculated under assumptions A1, A2, A3, and A4.*

*What produced the identity of results of the two models (parts A and B of the appendix) is the assumption that the meritorious are *less* easily deterred than the nonmeritorious. Consequently, the phenomenon reported by Atkinson and Micklewright (1991, 1693–94) that meritorious are deterred indicates that these people have a different preference profile from the one postulated here; either they have a dominant strategy of not applying (because of ignorance, for example) or are more easily deterred than the nonmeritorious (because they are more sensitive to the humiliation produced by scrutiny or by [an always possible] rejection).

NOTES

Financial support was provided to Tsebelis by the Hoover Institution and the Institute for Industrial Relations of UCLA, and to Stephen by the Center of International and Strategic Affairs of UCLA. We would like to thank Jeff Frieden and Douglas Ashford for useful comments.

1. The tests of conditions (a) to (d) for unemployment assistance may not be as stringent as for unemployment insurance; however, countries may link these benefits to reintegration in society (like the "revenu minimum d'insertion" in France).

2. Reported in Atkinson and Micklewright 1991, 1689.

3. The standard game-theoretic representation of the fact that the agency does not know whether a particular person is meritorious or not is a move by "nature" in the beginning of the game.

4. A very interesting argument along these lines has been offered by Atkinson and Mickelwright (1989) in order to account for the "turning of the screw" on British unemployed in the 1980s.

5. See appendix (part B) for the case where assumption 2 is replaced by assumption 2': $b_1 > c_1 > a'_1$ where $a'_1 > a_1$.

6. Our examination of the policies of various countries suggests that these two purposes are very often present at the same time and are pursued equally by governments of different political complexions. Our model implies that there is no analytical value gained by distinguishing between a left-wing or right-wing basis for workfare.

7. The reader can verify this statement by replacing p^* from equation (1) in this ratio.

8. A policy of monitoring was also made possible because of the improvements in the government's fiscal position. Government share of GDP peaked in the years 1982/83/84 and declined steadily thereafter (OECD 1991b, 68).

9. A problem with the index of left government used (see table 1 for a full definition) is that it only includes governments up to the end of the 1970s. However, due to the way participation in government is scored, change in the political composition of governments in the 1980s will not have a dramatic effect.

10. However, it is possible that monitoring is a function of the general level of government employment. Therefore we ran a multiple regression in which benefits and government employment as a share of GDP in each country were regressed against monitoring. The results in line 8 show that benefits remain significantly related, while the result for government employment is not significant.

References

Accornero, Aris, Fabrizio Carmignani, and Nino Magna. 1985. "I tre 'tipi^a di operai della Fiat." *Politica ed Economia* 16 (5): 33–47.

Adomeit, Hannes. 1994. "Gorbachev, German Unification and the Collapse of Empire." *Post-Soviet Affairs* 10 (3): 197–230.

Alba-Ramirez, A., and R. B. Freeman. 1990. "Job Finding and Wages When Longrun Unemployment Is Really Long: The Case of Spain." NBER Working Paper #3409.

Altshuler, Alan, Martin Anderson, and Daniel Jones. 1984. *The Future of the Automobile: The Report of MIT's International Automobile Program.* Cambridge: MIT Press.

Andersen, S. 1989. "Unemployment among Laid-off Shipyard Workers." Arhus Business School Working Papers, 89, #3.

Anderson, John C. 1979. "Local Union Participation: A Re-examination." *Industrial Relations* 18 (1): 18–31.

Anderson, Richard D., Jr. 1993. *Public Politics in an Authoritarian State: Making Foreign Policy during the Brezhnev Years.* Ithaca: Cornell University Press.

Asmus, Ronald D., J. F. Brown, and Keith Crane. 1991. *Soviet Foreign Policy and the Revolutions of 1989 in Eastern Europe.* Santa Monica, CA: RAND.

Atherton, Wallace N. 1973. *Theory of Union Bargaining Goals.* Princeton: Princeton University Press.

Atkinson, Anthony B., J. Gomulka, J. Micklewright, and N. Rau. 1984. "Unemployment Benefit, Duration and Incentives in Britain: How Robust Is the Evidence?" *Journal of Public Economics* 23:3–26.

Atkinson, Anthony B., and John Micklewright. 1985. "Unemployment Benefits and Unemployment Duration." STICERD. Occasional Paper #5. London: London School of Economics.

———. 1989. "Turning the Screw: Benefits for the Unemployed 1979–88." In Andrew Dilnot and Ian Walker, eds., *The Economics of Social Security.* Oxford: Oxford University Press.

———. 1991. "Unemployment Compensation and Labor Market Transitions: A Critical Review." *Journal of Economic Literature* 29:1679–1727.

Austen-Smith, David, and Jeffrey Banks. 1988. "Elections, Coalitions, and Legislative Outcomes." *American Political Science Review* 82:405–22.

Axelrod, Robert. 1970. *Conflict of Interest.* Chicago: Markham.

Babb, James. 1992. "The Statics and Dynamics of Japan Socialist Party Ideology." Paper presented at the annual meeting of the American Political Science Association, Chicago.

Bakke, Bente. 1990. *På Bakerste Benk.* Oslo: Aschehoug.

Baldissera, Alberto. 1984. "Alle origini della politica della disuguaglianza nell'Italia degli anni '80: la marcia dei quarantamila." *Quaderni di Sociologia* 31 (1): 1–78.

Baron, David P. 1991. "A Spatial Theory of Government Formation in Parliamentary Systems." *American Political Science Review* 85:137–64.

———. 1993. "Government Formation and Endogeneous Parties." *American Political Science Review* 87:34–47.

Barron, John, and Wesley Mellow. 1981. "Unemployment Insurance: The Recipients and Its Impact." *Southern Economic Journal* 47:606–16.

Bates, Robert H., Avner Greif, Margaret Levi, Jean-Laurent Rosenthal, and Barry R. Weingast. 1998a. *Analytical Narratives.* Princeton: Princeton University Press.

———. 1998b. "Introduction." In R. H. Bates et al., *Analytical Narratives.* Princeton: Princeton University Press.

Batstone, Eric, Ian Boraston, and Stephen Frenkel. 1977. *Shop Stewards in Action: The Organisation of Workplace Conflict and Accommodation.* Oxford: Basil Blackwell.

Bessone, Mario, et al. 1983. "Dossier Fiat Auto: il prezzo dei profitti." *Azimut* 2 (5): 104–22.

Bjorklund, A. 1990. "Unemployment, Labor Market Policy and Income Distribution." In I. Persson, ed., *Generating Equality in the Welfare State: The Swedish Experience.* Oslo: Norwegian University Press.

Bjorklund, A., and B. Holmlund. 1989. "Effects of Extended Unemployment Compensation in Sweden." In B. Gustafsson and N. Anders, eds., *The Political Economy of Social Security,* 165–81. Amsterdam: North Holland.

Blair, Douglas H., and David L. Crawford. 1984. "Labor Union Objectives and Collective Bargaining." *Quarterly Journal of Economics* 49:547–66.

Blank, Rebecca, and David Card. 1989. "Recent Trends in Insured and Uninsured Employment: Is There an Explanation?" NBER Working Paper #2871.

Bonazzi, Giuseppe. 1984. "La lotta dei 35 giorni alla Fiat: un'analisi sociologica." *Politica ed Economia* 15 (11): 33–43.

———. 1987. "Contrattare alla Fiat." *Prospettiva Sindacale* 18 (64): 76–82.

———. 1988. "La sociologia e il gioco della produzione." *Politica ed Economia* 19 (1): 3–6.

Breslauer, George W. 1989. "Evaluating Gorbachev as Leader." *Soviet Economy* 5: 299–340.

British Leyland (BL) Cars. 1980. "Final Draft of Proposed Agreement on Bargaining, Pay, Employee Benefits and Productivity, Covering Hourly Rated Employees in BL Cars." News-sheet distributed to manual employees.

British Motor Corporation (BMC). 1956. Press statement. Typescript dated July 19.

Brown, J. C. 1990. *Victims or Villains? Social Security Benefits and Unemployment.* London: Joseph Rowntree Trust.

Brown, J. F. 1988. *Eastern Europe and Communist Rule.* Durham, NC: Duke University Press.

Brunell, Thomas. 1999. Partisan Bias in U.S. Congressional Elections, 1952–96: Why the Senate Is Usually More Republican than the House of Representatives" *American Politics Quarterly* 27 (3): 316–37.

Brunell, Thomas, Bernard Grofman, and William Koetzle. 2000. "Six Puzzles about Congressional Elections." Typescript.

Brunhes, Bernard, and Denise Annandale-Massa. 1986. *L'Indemnisation du Chomage en Europe: Cinq Pays, Cinque Regimes.* Paris: l'UNEDIC.

Brzezinski, Zbigniew K. 1989. *The Grand Failure: The Birth and Death of Communism in the Twentieth Century.* New York: Scribner.

Budge, Ian, and Michael J. Laver. 1986. "Office Seeking and Policy Pursuit in Coalition Theory." *Legislative Studies Quarterly* 11:485–506.

Bundesminister für Arbeit und Sozialordnung (BAS). 1990. *Sozialbericht 1990.* Bonn: BAS.

Calmfors, Lars, and John Driffill. 1988. "Bargaining Structure, Corporatism, and Macroeconomic Performance." Economic Policy 3 (2): 14–61.

Calvert, Randall L. 1987. "Reputation and Legislative Leadership." *Public Choice* 55:81–119.

Cameron, David. 1984. "Social Democracy, Corporatism, Labour Quiescence, and the Representation of Economic Interest in Advanced Capitalist Society." In *Order and Conflict in Contemporary Capitalism: Studies in the Political Economy of Western European Nations*, ed. John H. Goldthorpe. New York: Oxford University Press.

Carmignani, Fabrizio. 1984. "Il 'sindacato di classe^a nella lotta dei 35 giorni alla Fiat." *Politica ed Economia* 15 (11): 43–48.

Carroll, John S. 1980. "Analyzing Decision Behavior: The Magician's Audience." In Thomas S. Wallsten, ed., *Cognitive Processes in Choice and Decision Behavior.* Hillsdale, NJ: Lawrence Erlbaum.

Centre for Policy Studies. 1983. *BL: Changing Gear.* London: Centre for Policy Studies.

Cherniaev, Andrei S. 1993. *Shest' let s Gorbachevym: Po dnevnikovym zapisiam.* Moscow: "Kul'tura."

Christensen, Raymond V. 1996. "Strategic Imperatives of Japan's SNTV Electoral System and the Cooperative Innovations of the Former Opposition Parties." *Comparative Political Studies* 29 (3): 312–34.

Christensen, Raymond V., and Paul E. Johnson. 1995. "Toward a Context Rich Analysis of Electoral Systems: The Japanese Example." *American Journal of Political Science* 39:575–98.

Clark, Kim, and Lawrence Summers. 1982. "Unemployment Insurance and Labor Market Transitions." In Martin N. Baily, ed., *Workers, Jobs and Inflation,* 279–318. Washington, DC: Brookings Institution.

Clegg, Hugh Armstrong. 1979. *The Changing System of Industrial Relations in Great Britain.* Oxford: Basil Blackwell.

Collier, David. 1999. "Building a Disciplined, Rigorous Center in Comparative Politics." *Newsletter of the Organized Section in Comparative Politics of the American Political Science Association* 10, no. 2 (summer): 1–2, 4.

Comito, Vicenzo. 1982. *La Fiat tra crisi e ristrutturazione.* Rome: Editori Riuniti.

Cox, Gary W. 1987. "Electoral Equilibrium under Alternative Voting Institutions." *American Journal of Political Science* 31:82–108.

———. 1990. "Centripetal and Centrifugal Incentives in Electoral Systems." *American Journal of Political Science* 34:903–35.

———. 1994. "Strategic Voting Equilibria under the Single Nontransferable Vote." *American Political Science Review* 88:608–21.

———. 1996. "Is the Single Non-transferable Vote Superproportional?" *American Journal of Political Science* 40:740–55.

Cox, Gary W., and Samuel Kernell. 1991. "Conclusion." In *The Politics of Divided Government,* Gary W. Cox and Samuel Kernell, eds. Boulder: Westview Press.

Crombez, Cristophe. 1996. "Minority Governments, Minimum Winning Coalitions, and Surplus Majorities in Parliamentary Systems." *European Journal of Political Research* 29:1–29.

Curtis, Gerald. 1988. *The Japanese Way of Politics.* New York: Columbia University Press.

Dagbladet. 1987. June 17.

Danziger, Sheldon, Robert H. Haveman, and Robert Plotnick. 1981. "How Income Transfer Programs Affect Work, Savings and Income Distribution: A Critical Review." *Journal of Economic Literature* 19:975–1028.

Davidson, Chandler, and Bernard Grofman, eds. 1994. *Quiet Revolution in the South: The Impact of the Voting Rights Act, 1965–1990.* Princeton: Princeton University Press.

De Menil, George. 1971. *Bargaining: Monopoly Power versus Union Power.* Cambridge: MIT Press.

De Swaan, Abram. 1973. *Coalition Theories and Cabinet Formation.* Amsterdam: Elsevier.

Dealessandri, Tom, and Maurizio Magnabosco. 1987. *Contrattare alla Fiat. Quindici anni di relazioni sindacali,* ed. Carlo Degiacomi. Rome: Edizioni Lavoro.

Department of Social Security (DSS). 1990. *Department of Social Security: Annual Report, 1989–90.* Canberra: Australian Government Publishing Service.

Department of Social Welfare (DSW). 1988. *Guide: Social Welfare Services.* Dublin: Department of Social Welfare.

———. 1990. *Statistical Information on Social Welfare Services 1989.* Dublin: The Stationery Office.

Dina, Angelo. 1981. "Fiat: i '35 giorni[a] e dopo." *Classe* 12 (19): 5–36.

Dodd, Lawrence C. 1976. *Coalitions in Parliamentary Government.* Princeton: Princeton University Press.

Downs, Anthony. 1957. *An Economic Theory of Democracy.* New York: Harper and Row.

Edwardes, Michael. 1983. *Back from the Brink: An Apocalyptic Experience.* London: Pan.

Elster, Jon. 1984. *Ulysses and the Sirens.* Cambridge: Cambridge University Press.

———. 1992. *Local Justice: How Institutions Allocate Scarce Goods and Necessary Burdens.* New York: Russell Sage Foundation.

Federazione CGIL-CISL-UIL Piemonte. 1980. "Fiat storia di una lotta." *Bollettino Mensile di Documentazione,* no. 36.

Federazione Lavoratori Metalmeccanici (FLM) Piemonte, ufficio informazioni. N.d. [ca. 1980]. "Memoria storica delle lotte Fiat." Unpublished document.

Fischhoff, Baruch. 1982. "For Those Condemned to Study the Past: Heuristics and Biases in Hindsight." In Daniel Kahneman, Paul Slovic, and A. Tversky, eds., *Judgment under Uncertainty: Heuristics and Biases.* Cambridge: Cambridge University Press.

Flanagan, Scott C. 1984. "Electoral Change in Japan: A Study of Secular Realignment."

In Russell J. Dalton et al., eds., *Electoral Change in Advanced Industrial Democracies,* 159–204. Princeton: Princeton University Press.

Florens, Jean-Pierre, Louis-André Gérard-Varet, and Patrick Werquin. 1990a. "The Duration of Current and Complete Unemployment Spells between 1984 and 1986 in France: Modelling and Empirical Evidence." In Jean-Pierre Florens, Marc Ivaldi, Jean-Jacques Laffont, and François Laisney, eds., *Microeconometrics: Surveys and Applications,* 302–43. Oxford: Basil Blackwell.

Florens, Jean-Pierre, D. Fougere, and P. Werquin. 1990b. "Durées de Chomage et Transitions sur le Marche du Travail." *Sociologie du Travail* 32:4.

Fudenberg, Drew, and Jean Tirole. 1991. *Game Theory.* Cambridge: MIT Press.

Geddes, Barbara. 1990. "How the Cases You Choose Affect the Answers You Get: Selection Bias in Comparative Politics." In *Political Analysis,* vol. 2., ed. James A. Stimson. Ann Arbor: University of Michigan Press.

Gekkan Shakai-to Henshu-bu. 1974. *Nihon Shakai-to no Sanjyu-nen* (1). Tokyo: Shakai-to Kikanshi-kyoku.

Golden, Miriam A. 1988. *Labor Divided: Austerity and Working-Class Politics in Contemporary Italy.* Ithaca: Cornell University Press.

———. 1989. "Le sconfitte eroiche della classe operaia." *Politica ed Economia* 20 (1): 33–44.

Gooding, John. 1990. "Gorbachev and Democracy." *Soviet Studies* 42:195–231.

Green, Donald, and Ian Shapiro. 1994. *Pathologies of Rational Choice: A Critique of Applications in Political Science.* New Haven: Yale University Press.

Grofman, Bernard. 1993a. "Is Turnout the Paradox That Ate Rational Choice Theory?" In *Information, Participation, and Choice,* 93–103. Ann Arbor: University of Michigan Press.

———, ed. 1993b. *Information, Participation, and Choice: 'An Economic Theory of Democracy' in Perspective.* Ann Arbor, Michigan: University of Michigan Press.

———. 1993c. "On the Gentle Art of Rational Choice Bashing." In Bernard Grofman, ed., *Information, Participation, and Choice: 'An Economic Theory of Democracy' in Perspective,* 239–42. Ann Arbor: University of Michigan Press.

———. 1996. "Political Economy: Downsian Perspectives." In Robert Goodin and Hans-Dieter Klingemann, eds., *New Handbook of Political Science,* 691–701. New York and London: Oxford University Press.

Ham, John, and Samuel Rea. 1987. "Unemployment Insurance and Male Unemployment Duration in Canada." *Journal of Labor Economics* 5:325–53.

Hellman, Stephen. 1988. *Italian Communism in Transition: The Rise and Fall of the Historic Compromise in Turin, 1975–1980.* New York: Oxford University Press.

Hey, John. 1979. *Uncertainty in Microeconomics.* Oxford: Martin Robertson.

Hirsch, Barry T., and John T. Addison. 1986. *The Economic Analysis of Unions: New Approaches and Evidence.* Boston: Allen and Unwin.

Hough, Jerry F. 1989. "The Politics of Successful Economic Reform." *Soviet Economy* 5:3–46.

Hujer, Reinhard, and Hilmar Schneider. 1989. "The Analysis of Labor Market Mobility Using Panel Data." *European Economic Review* 33:530–36.

Huszczo, Gregory E. 1983. "Attitudinal and Behavioral Variables Related to Participation in Union Activities." *Journal of Labor Research* 4 (3): 289–97.

International Labor Organization (ILO). 1986. *Employment Protection and Social Security, Report IV* (1). Geneva: ILO.

Ishikawa, Masumi. 1995. *Sengo Seiji-shi*. Tokyo: Iwanami.

Jefferys, Steve. 1988. "The Changing Face of Conflict: Shopfloor Organization at Longbridge, 1939–1980." In *Shopfloor Politics and Job Controls: The Post-War Engineering Industry*, ed. Michael Terry and P. K. Edwards. Oxford: Basil Blackwell.

Johnson, G. E., and R. Layard. 1986. "The Natural Rate of Unemployment: Explanation and Policy." In O. Ashenfelter and R. Layard, eds., *Handbook of Labor Economic*, 921–99. Amsterdam: North-Holland.

Jones, Daniel T. 1983. "Technology and the UK Automobile Industry." *Lloyds Bank Review* 148:14–27.

Jones, D. T., and S. J. Prais. 1978. "Plant-Size and Productivity in the Motor Industry: Some International Comparisons." *Oxford Bulletin of Economics and Statistics* 40 (2): 131–51.

Karasch, Jurgen. 1983. "Der Begriff der 'Zumutbarkeit' im Wandel der Rechtsauffassungen vom AVAVG 1927 bis zum AFKG 1982." In *Zentralblatt für Sozialversicherung Sozialhilfe und Versorgung* 37:66–72.

Katz, Lawrence, and Bruce D. Meyer. 1990. "Unemployment Insurance, Recall Expectations and Unemployment Outcomes." NBER Working Paper #2594.

Katzenstein, Peter. 1985. *Small States in World Markets: Industrial Policy in Europe*. Ithaca: Cornell University Press.

Kerschen, Nicole, and Francis Kessler. 1990. "Unemployment Benefit in France and the Federal Republic of Germany: Social Protection or Employment Market Regulation? Some Legal Aspects." *International Social Security Review* 43:270–86.

King, Desmond S., and Hugh Ward. 1992. "Working for Benefits: Rational Choice and the Rise of Work-Welfare Programmes." *Political Studies* 15:475–95.

Kohno, Masaru. 1994. "Sengo Nihon no Seito Sisutemu no Henka to Gouri-teki Sentaku." In Nihon Seiji Gakkai, ed., *Nempo Seijigaku*. Tokyo: Iwanami.

———. 1997. *Japan's Postwar Party Politics*. Princeton: Princeton University Press.

Korpi, Walter, and Michael Shalev. 1980. "Strikes, Power and Politics in the Western Nations, 1900–1976." *Political Power and Social Theory: A Research Annual*, ed. Maurice Zeitlin. Vol. 1. Greenwich, CT: JAI.

Kreps, David M. 1990. "Corporate Culture and Economic Theory." In *Perspectives on Positive Political Economy*, James E. Alt and Kenneth A. Shepsle, eds. Cambridge: Cambridge University Press.

Lancaster, T., and S. J. Nickell. 1980. "The Analysis of the Re-employment Probabilities for the Unemployed." *Journal of the Royal Statistical Society* 143:555–66.

Lange, Peter, and Geoffrey Garrett. 1985. "The Politics of Growth: Strategic Interaction and Economic Performance in the Advanced Industrial Democracies, 1974–1980." *Journal of Politics* 47:792–827.

Laver, Michael J., and Norman Schofield. 1990. *Multiparty Government: The Politics of Coalition in Europe*. Oxford: Oxford University Press.

Laver, Michael J., and Kenneth A. Shepsle. 1990a. "Coalitions and Cabinet Government." *American Political Science Review* 84:873–90.

———. 1990b. "Government Coalitions and Intraparty Politics." *British Journal of Political Science* 20:489–507.

Law, Christopher M. 1985. "The Geography of Industrial Rationalisation: The British Motor Car Assembly Industry, 1972–1982." *Geography* 70 (1): 1–12.

Leiserson, Michael. 1968. "Factions and Coalitions in One-Party Japan." *American Political Science Review* 62:770–87.

Leyland Combine Trade Union Committee. N.d. [ca. November 1979]. "British Leyland, The Edwardes Plan and Your Job." Pamphlet distributed to employees.

Ligachev, Egor. 1993. *Inside Gorbachev's Kremlin.* Translated from the Russian by Catherine A. Fitzpatrick, Michele A. Berdy, and Dobrochna Dyrcz-Freeman. New York: Pantheon.

Lippman, Steven, and John McCall. 1979. *Studies in the Economics of Search.* Amsterdam: North-Holland.

Lowenthal, Richard. 1974. "On 'Established' Communist Regimes." *Studies in Comparative Communism* 4:335–58.

Luebbert, Gregory M. 1983. "Coalition Theory and Government Formation in Multiparty Democracies." *Comparative Politics* 15:235–49.

———. 1986. *Comparative Democracy: Policymaking and Governing Coalitions in Europe and Israel.* New York: Columbia University Press.

Maier, Charles S. 1997. *Dissolution: The Crisis of Communism and the End of East Germany.* Princeton: Princeton University Press.

Marer, Paul. 1984. "The Political Economy of Soviet Relations with Eastern Europe." In Sarah Meiklejohn Terry, ed., *Soviet Policy in Eastern Europe.* New Haven: Yale University Press.

Marrese, Michael, and Jan Vanous. 1983. *Soviet Subsidization of Trade with Eastern Europe: A Soviet Perspective.* Berkeley: Institute of International Studies.

———. 1988. "The Content and Controversy of Soviet Trade Relations with Eastern Europe." In Josef C. Brada, Ed A. Hewett, and Thomas A. Wolf, eds., *Economic Adjustment and Reform in Eastern Europe and the Soviet Union: Essays in Honor of Franklyn D. Holzman.* Durham, NC: Duke University Press.

Marsden, David, Timothy Morris, Paul Willman, and Stephen Wood. 1985. *The Car Industry: Labour Relations and Industrial Adjustment.* London: Tavistock.

McCubbins, Mathew D., and Frances McCall Rosenbluth. 1995. "Party Provision for Personal Politics: Dividing the Vote in Japan." In Peter F. Cowhey and Mathew D. McCubbins, eds., *Structure and Policy in Japan and the United States.* New York: Cambridge University Press.

McDonald, Ian M., and Robert M. Solow. 1981. "Wage Bargaining and Employment." *American Economic Review* 71 (5): 896–908.

Mershon, Carol. 1996. "The Costs of Coalition—Coalition Theories and Italian Governments." *American Political Science Review* 90, no. 3 (September): 534–54.

Micklewright, John. 1985. "On Earnings-related Unemployment Benefits and Their Relation to Earnings." *Economic Journal* 95:133–45.

———. 1990. "Why Do Less than a Quarter of the Unemployed in Britain Receive Unemployment Insurance?" European U. Working Paper in Economics, Florence and TIDI Program Discussion Paper 147, STICERD, London School of Economics.

Mizuno, A. 1989. "Characteristics and Behavior of Unemployment Insurance Beneficiaries." *Economi   dies* 30:3 (Chuo University, in Japanese).

Mlynar, Zdenek. 1980. *Nightfrost in Prague: The End of Humane Socialism.* Trans. by Paul Wilson. New York: Karz.

Moffitt, R. A. 1985. "Unemployment Insurance and the Distribution of Unemployment Spells." *Journal of Econometrics* 28:85–101.

Moffitt, R. A., and W. Nicholson. 1982. "The Effect of Unemployment Insurance on Unemployment: The Case of Federal Supplemental Benefits." *Review of Economics and Statistics* 64 (1):1–11.

Narendranathan, W., S. J. Nickell, and J. Stern. 1985. "Unemployment Benefits Revisited." *Economic Journal* 95:307–29.

Nickell, Stephen J. 1979a. "Estimating the Probability of Leaving Unemployment." *Econometrica* 47:1249–66.

———. 1979b. "The Effect of Unemployment and Related Benefits on the Duration of Unemployment." *Economic Journal* 89:34–49.

Norvik, Erling. 1990. *Hiv Dokker i Kalosjan.* Oslo: J. W. Cappelen.

OECD. 1988. *Employment Outlook.* Paris: OECD.

———. 1990. *Labour Market Policies for the 1990s.* Paris: OECD.

———. 1991a. *Employment Outlook.* Paris: OECD.

———. 1991b. *Historical Statistics: 1960–1989.* Paris: OECD.

Oswald, Andrew J. 1986a. "Is Wage Rigidity Caused by 'Layoffs by Seniority'?" In *Wage Rigidity and Unemployment,* ed. Wilfred Beckerman. Baltimore: Johns Hopkins University Press.

———. 1986b. "Wage Determination and Recession: A Report on Recent Work." *British Journal of Industrial Relations* 24:181–94.

Otake, Hideo. 1986. "Nihon Shakai-to Higeki no Kigen." *Chuo Koron* (October): 146–61.

———. 1988. *Sai-Gunbi to Nashonarizumu.* Tokyo: Chuo Koron-sha.

Padoa-Schioppa, Fiorella. 1988. "Underemployment Benefit Effects on Employment and Income Distribution: What We Should Learn from the System of the *Cassa Integrazione Guadagni.*" *Labour* 2 (2): 101–24.

Pal, Leslie A. 1988. *State, Class and Bureaucracy: Canadian Unemployment Insurance and Public Policy.* Montreal: McGill-Queen's University Press.

Palfrey, Thomas. 1984. "Spatial Equilibrium with Entry." *Review of Economic Studies* 51:139–56.

Perline, Martin, and V. R. Lorenz. 1970. "Factors Influencing Member Participation in Trade Union Activities." *American Journal of Economics and Sociology* 29 (4): 425–38.

Pridham, Geoffrey, ed. 1986. *Coalition Behaviour in Theory and Practice.* Cambridge: Cambridge University Press.

Ramseyer, J. Mark, and Frances McCall Rosenbluth. 1993. *Japan's Political Market Place.* Cambridge: Harvard University Press.

Rasmusen, Eric. 1989. *Games and Information: An Introduction to Game Theory.* Oxford: Basil Blackwell.

Reed, Steven R. 1991. "Structure and Behaviour: Extending Duverger's Law to the Japanese Case." *British Journal of Political Science* 29:335–56.

Reed, Steven R., and John M. Bolland. 1991. "The Fragmentation Effect of SNTV in Japan." Paper presented at the conference on Election Systems in Japan, Korea,

Taiwan, and Alabama in Comparative Perspectives, University of California, Irvine, February.

Rhodes, Martin, and Vincent Wright. 1988. "The European Steel Unions and the Steel Crisis, 1974–84: A Study in the Demise of Traditional Unionism." *British Journal of Political Science* 18 (2): 171–95.

Riker, William H. 1962. *The Theory of Political Coalitions.* New Haven: Yale University Press.

———. 1976. "The Number of Political Parties: A Reexamination of Duverger's Law." *Comparative Politics* 9:93–106.

———. 1980. "Implications from the Disequilibrium of Majority Rule for the Study of Institutions." *American Political Science Review* 74:432–46.

———. 1982. "The Two-Party System and Duverger's Law: An Essay on the History of Political Science." *American Political Science Review* 76:753–66.

Roeder, Philip G. 1993. *Red Sunset: The Failure of Soviet Politics.* Princeton University Press.

Romiti, Cesare. 1988. *Questi anni alla Fiat.* Interview by Giampaolo Pansa. Milan: Rizzoli.

Rommetvedt, Hilmar. 1987. "Velgerbevegelser i fir faster." *Folkets Framtid,* October 30.

———. 1991. "Partiavstand og partikoalisjoner." Dissertation, University of Bergen.

Rubinstein, Alvin Z. 1988. *Moscow's Third World Strategy.* Princeton: Princeton University Press.

Salmon, John. 1983. "Organised Labour in a Market Economy: A Study of Redundancy and Workplace Relations as an Issue of Power-Conflict in the British Motor Industry." Ph.D. dissertation, University of Warwick.

———. 1988. "Wage Strategy, Redundancy and Shop Stewards in the Coventry Motor Industry." In *Shopfloor Politics and Job Controls: The Post-War Engineering Industry,* ed. Michael Terry and P. K. Edwards. Oxford: Basil Blackwell.

Sato, Seizaburo, and Tetsuhisa Matsuzaki. 1986. *Jiminto Seiken.* Tokyo: Chuo Koron-sha.

Scarbrough, Harry. 1982. "The Control of Technological Change in the Motor Industry: A Case Study." 2 vols. Ph.D. dissertation, Aston University, Birmingham.

———. 1986. "The Politics of Technological Change at British Leyland." In *Technological Change, Rationalisation and Industrial Relations,* ed. Otto Jacobi et al. London: Croom Helm.

Seglow, Peter, and Patricia Wallace. 1984. "Trade Unions and Change in the British Car Industry." Research Paper 84/2. London: Policy Studies Institute.

Selten, Reinhard. 1975. "Reexamination of the Perfectness Concept for Equilibrium Points in Extensive Games." *International Journal of Game Theory* 4:25–55.

Services des Études et de la Statistique (SES). 1986. *Tableaux Statistiques: Travail, Emploi, Formation Professionelle.* Paris: Ministère du Travail, de l'Emploi et de la Formation Professionelle.

Shevardnadze, Eduard. 1991. *Moi vybor: v zashchitu demokratii i svobody.* Moscow: Novosti.

Spinrad, William. 1960. "Correlates of Trade Union Participation: A Summary of the Literature." *American Sociological Review* 25:237–44.

Standing, Guy. 1988. *Unemployment and Labor Market Flexibility: Sweden.* Geneva: International Labor Office.

Stockwin, J. A. A. 1968. *The Japanese Socialist Party and Neutralism.* Carlton, Australia: Melbourne University Press.

———. 1986. "The Japan Socialist Party: A Politics of Permanent Opposition." In Ronald Hrebenar, ed., *The Japanese Party System: From One-Party Rule to Coalition Government.* Boulder: Westview Press.

Stortingstidende 1986–87, 4082–4214.

Streeck, Wolfgang. 1985. "Introduction: Industrial Relations, Technical Change and Economic Restructuring." In "Industrial Relations and Technical Change in the British, Italian and German Automobile Industry:" Three Case Studies, Wolfgang Streeck, ed. Discussion paper IIM/LMP 85-5. Berlin: Wissenschaftszentrum.

Streeck, Wolfgang, and Andreas Hoff. 1983. "Manpower Management and Industrial Relations in the Restructuring of the World Automobile Industry." Discussion paper IIM/LMP 83-35. Berlin: Wissenschaftszentrum.

Strøm, Kaare. 1990a. "A Behavioral Theory of Competitive Political Parties." *American Journal of Political Science* 34:565–98.

———. 1990b. *Minority Government and Majority Rule.* New York: Cambridge University Press.

———. 1993. "Competition Ruins the Good Life: Party Leadership in Norway." *European Journal of Political Research* 24 (3): 317–47.

Strøm, Kaare, Ian Budge, and Michael J. Laver. 1994. "Constraints on Government Formation in Multiparty Democracies." *American Journal of Political Science* 38 (2): 303–35.

Strøm, Kaare, and Jørn Y. Leipart. 1993. "Policy, Institutions, and Coalition Avoidance: Norwegian Governments, 1945–1990." *American Political Science Review* 87: 870–87.

Taylor, Michael. 1987. *The Possibility of Cooperation.* Cambridge: Cambridge University Press.

Taylor, Stan. 1981. "De-industrialization and Unemployment in the West Midlands." In *Unemployment,* ed. Bernard Crick. London: Methuen.

Thomassen, Petter. 1991. *En Regjerings Fall.* Oslo: J. W. Cappelen.

Treu, Tiziano. 1982. "Italy." In *Workforce Reductions in Undertakings: Policies and Measures for the Protection of Redundant Workers in Seven Industrialized Market Economy Countries,* ed. Edward Yemin. Geneva: International Labour Office.

Trivedi, Pravin K., and Cesari Kapuscinski. 1985. "Determinants of Inflow into Unemployment and the Probability of Leaving Unemployment: A Desegregated Analysis." In P. Volcker, ed., *The Structure and Duration of Unemployment in Australia,* 151–85. BLMR Monograph #6. Canberra: Australian Government Publishing Service.

Tsebelis, George. 1989. "The Abuse of Probability in Political Analysis: The Robinson Crusoe Fallacy." *American Political Science Review* 83:77–91.

———. 1990a. *Nested Games: Rational Choice in Comparative Politics.* Berkeley: University of California Press.

———. 1990b. "Penalty Has No Impact On Crime: A Game-Theoretic Analysis." *Rationality and Society* 2:255–86.

U.S. Department of Health and Human Services. 1989. "Social Security Programs in the United States." *Social Security Bulletin* 52:2–79.

Van den Berg, Gerard. 1990. "Non-stationarity in Job Search Theory." *Review of Econometric Studies* 57:255–77.

Ventura, Luciano. 1990. "Licenziamenti collettivi." In *Enciclopedia guiridica treccani,* vol. 19. Rome: Treccani.

Walker, Bruce. 1987. "Changes in the UK Motor Industry: An Analysis of Some Local Economic Impacts." Motor Industry Local Authority Network in association with the Institute of Local Government Studies, University of Birmingham.

Weingast, Barry. 1996. "Formal Theory and Comparative Politics." Presented at the Annual Meeting of the American Political Science Association, San Francisco.

Wilensky, Harold L. 1981. "Leftism, Catholicism, and Democratic Corporatism: The Role of Political Parties in Recent Welfare State Development." Peter Flora and Arnold J. Heidenheimer, eds., *The Development of Welfare States in Europe and America.* New Brunswick, NJ: Transaction Books.

Wilks, Stephen. 1984. *Industrial Policy and the Motor Industry.* Manchester: Manchester University Press.

Willman, Paul. 1984. "The Reform of Collective Bargaining and Strike Activity in BL Cars 1976–1982." *Industrial Relations Journal* 15 (2): 6–17.

Willman, Paul, and Graham Winch. 1985. *Innovation and Management Control: Labour Relations at BL Cars.* Cambridge: Cambridge University Press.

Willoch, Kåre I. 1990. *Statsminister.* Oslo: Chr. Schibsted.

Wilson, James Q. 1973. *Political Organizations.* New York: Basic Books.

Wuffle, A. 1999. "Credo of a 'Reasonable Choice' Modeler." *Journal of Theoretical Politics* 11 (2): 203–6.

Wurzel, Eckard. 1988. "Unemployment Duration in West Germany—An Analysis of Grouped Data." Institut für Stabielierungs und Strukturpolitik. University of Bonn, Working Paper, 88/2.

Zelikow, Philip, and Condoleeza Rice. 1995. *Germany Reunified and Europe Transformed: A Study in Statecraft.* Cambridge: Harvard University Press.

Contributors

RICHARD D. ANDERSON JR. is associate professor of political science at the University of California at Los Angeles. He has published on the politics of Soviet foreign and defense policy. As the Soviet Union began to disintegrate, his research shifted to the potential of linguistics to inform the study of electoral polities, with Russia as the example on which his research concentrates. Before returning to earn a doctorate at the University of California, Berkeley, he worked as an analyst of Soviet military policy for the CIA and as a member of the staff of the Oversight Subcommittee of the House Permanent Select Committee on Intelligence.

MIRIAM A. GOLDEN is professor of political science at the University of California at Los Angeles. She is the author of *Heroic Defeats: The Politics of Job Loss* (1997). With Peter Lange and Michael Wallerstein, she is currently completing a book presenting and analyzing a data set compiled by the authors on unions, employers, industrial relations, and collective bargaining in sixteen OECD countries in the postwar era.

BERNARD GROFMAN is professor of political science and social psychology at the University of California, Irvine. He is a specialist in the theory of representation. His major fields of interest are in American politics, comparative election systems, and social choice theory. He is coauthor, with Lisa Handley and Richard N. Niemi, of *Minority Representation and the Quest for Voting Equality* (1992), and he has also edited a number of books including *Choosing an Electoral System* (coedited with Arend Lijphart, 1984); *Electoral Laws and Their Political Consequences* (coedited with Arend Lijphart, 1986); *Information Pooling and Group Decision Making* (coedited with Guillermo Owen, 1986); *The Federalist Papers and the New Institutionalism* (coedited with Donald Wittman, 1989); *Political Gerrymandering and the Courts* (1990); *Controversies in Minority Voting: The Voting Rights Act in Perspective* (coedited with Chandler Davidson, 1992); *Information, Participation and Choice: An Economic Theory of Democracy in Perspective* (1995); *Quiet Revolution in the South: The Impact of the Voting Rights Act, 1965–1990* (coedited with Chandler Davidson, 1994); *Race and Redistricting in the 1990s* (1998); and *Japan, Korea, and Taiwan under the Single Non-Transferable Vote: The Comparative Study of an Embedded Institution* (coedited with Sung-Chull Lee, Edwin A. Winckler, and Brian Woodall, 1999).

MASARU KOHNO is associate professor of political science at Aoyama Gakuin University of Tokyo. He received a Bachelor of Laws degree from Sophia University (Tokyo), an M.A. degree in international relations from Yale University, and a Ph.D. degree in political science from Stanford University. He has published many articles on Japanese politics and foreign policy in a variety of journals both in English and Japanese, including *British Journal of Political Science, Comparative Politics, Leviathan*, and *World Politics*. He is the author of *Japan's Postwar Party Politics* (1997) and was a 1996–97 National Fellow at Hoover Institution, Stanford University.

ROLAND STEPHEN is assistant professor of political science at North Carolina State University. He received a B.A. in economics and history from Cambridge University and a Ph.D. in political science from the University of California at Los Angeles. He is the author of *Vehicle of Influence: Building a European Political Economy* (2000). His research is focused on the role played by institutions in international and comparative political economy.

KAARE STRØM is professor of political science at the University of California, San Diego. He received his Ph.D. from Stanford University in 1984. Strøm's research focuses on political parties, coalition bargaining, and the institutions of parliamentary democracy. His recent work includes *Challenges to Political Parties: The Case of Norway*, with Lars Svaasand (1997), *Koalitionsregierungen in Westeuropa*, with Wolfgang C. Mueller (1997), and *Policy, Office, or Votes: How Political Parties in Western Europe Make Hard Choices*, with Wolfgang C. Mueller (1999).

GEORGE TSEBELIS is professor of political science at the University of California at Los Angeles. He holds doctorates from Paris VI University in mathematical statistics and Washington University (St. Louis) in political science. He has published *Nested Games* (1990) and *Bicameralism* (coauthored with Jeannette Money, 1997). He has also published numerous articles in *American Political Science Review, British Journal of Political Science, International Organization, Journal of Theoretical Politics, Rationality and Society, International Political Science Review, International Review of Law and Economics, Journal of Legislative Studies,* and so on. His current work focuses on the institutions of the European Union, as well as comparisons across political systems with diverse institutional characteristics, such as presidential versus parliamentary, unicameral versus bicameral, and two versus multiparty.

Index